BETTER THAN LIFTING THINGS

GLENN SHEELEY

Back cover photo of Glenn Sheeley and Tom McCollister by Piper Jones Castillo.

Cover design and formatting by Stacey Blake, Champagne Book Design, Orlando, Fla.

Special acknowledgement to Stephan Rosenfeld, Identity Advisors/Strategic Communications, Jenkintown, Pa., for his generous and invaluable assistance with this book.

To my dearest Nora, who urged me to complete this book. While I can't promise you the screenplay and the movie, at least you already have your beach house.

To my daughters, Jessica and Katie, and our grandchildren, Tyler, Bryan, Luke, and Lucy, for making Grandpa my favorite occupation.

To Mom and Dad, Russ and Lori, who supported me, laughed with me, and left me too soon.

CONTENTS

FOREWORD
BY TERRY BRADSHAW

G LENN SHEELEY AND I WERE STILL KIDS IN OUR 20S WHEN HE took over the Steelers beat for the *Pittsburgh Press* in 1976.

I had seen him around the team a little the year before, when he was helping Phil Musick cover us on the way to our second straight Super Bowl win, but when Glenn showed up at training camp that following summer as the main guy for the *Press,* I really didn't know what to expect.

He was another darned Yankee, of course, and I'd heard from Franco (Harris) that he went to Penn State, but I didn't hold that against him. He wrote some funny stuff, and he seemed like a fair reporter. He wasn't one of those guys who would just tear somebody apart for no reason. Especially me, and back then it felt like everybody was ripping me for something.

Truth is, Glenn ended up being about the only Pittsburgh writer back then that I really liked and enjoyed. We had a good relationship—or as good as you could have, I guess, with an athlete and a writer—and I remember thinking, I like this guy, I'll see if maybe I can get him on my side. I guess maybe I was able to because I can't ever remember being mad at him for anything he wrote.

Sometimes I would even stop by the press room at training camp after evening team meetings and shoot the breeze with him. There was usually nobody else in there, and I was interested in what he was thinking about the team, too. In the process, I tried to give him some inside stuff, usually talking off the record, and Glenn never violated that trust. That meant a lot to me.

After Glenn left Pittsburgh (in 1979) to work in Atlanta (for the *Journal-Constitution*), we saw each other occasionally around the NFL when I was first working for CBS, and then FOX. And, of course, when I was inducted into the Hall of Fame in 1989. But a few years ago, we reconnected again through our mutual friend, John Czarnecki, who worked with me for many years at FOX in Los Angeles after his newspaper career. Now Glenn and I talk every so often on the phone about golf, grandkids, and our health, plus often reminiscing about the many memories we share from Pittsburgh.

I only found out recently that we're both cancer survivors. Glenn had kidney cancer a long time ago (1998) and I've had my issues in recent years. Thank God we're both around to talk about them.

I was really happy to hear that Glenn had decided to complete this book. I knew he'd been working on it for quite some time and I'm glad it's finally out there for people to see. When he sent me my chapter a while back, I really enjoyed it and happily replied to him, "You've still got it."

As you might know, Glenn also had a long writing career in golf after leaving the NFL beat, and I've always loved golf, too, or at least until my body stopped remembering how to make a decent shoulder turn.

It wasn't easy covering the Steelers back in the '70s. You had to be there to really appreciate the craziness. People in hard hats, wearing our jerseys all over town. Black and gold everywhere you looked. The love affair between Pittsburgh and the Steelers was incredible. For the first couple of years after I got there, we were still lousy, and then suddenly we were Super Bowl champions. It seemed like it happened overnight.

I never really thought about it until Glenn asked me to write this foreword, but I guess there was a lot of pressure on him, too, having never covered a pro team before and starting with a two-time Super Bowl champion. Heck, nobody in Pittsburgh wanted to read about anything else, and back then, newspapers were still a big deal. Now it's all TV, but in the 1970s what was said about you in the paper was just as important as what the TV guys said on Sunday.

In those days, the writers even flew with us on the Steelers' team charter. I wasn't crazy about it—I felt that was our place to be, not theirs—but Mr. Rooney wanted all those guys from the smaller papers around Pittsburgh to enjoy the Steelers' success, too, after putting up with the team in the old days, and they couldn't have gotten to the road games any other way. Plus, it always gave me a chance to stop by Glenn's seat while he was trying to write on the plane and give him some grief.

We also shared our mutual frustration with Chuck Noll. Most everybody knows the issues I had with my head coach, but the media guys also had their problems with him. He was often cold to them, too, and considering how friendly everyone else was in the entire organization, Chuck's aloofness often made it difficult for everyone.

The complete opposite, of course, was Art Rooney, Sr., The Chief. Everybody loved that man, and we cherished the time we were able to spend with him. When I got to Pittsburgh, The Chief was somebody I could always talk to, even in the bad times, and I always appreciated that more than he probably ever knew.

I'm glad I could help out Glenn a little bit by writing this foreword. It's only fitting since he wrote such a nice review for me on the book jacket of my second book, *Looking Deep*. Heck, he even liked my 2020 COVID song, "Quarantine Crazy"—which, by the way, should have been a hit—and he owned a copy of my first re-cord album, *I'm So Lonesome I Could Cry*. I sure hope he didn't have to pay for it.

Now, here we are, all these years later. Glenn's retired and I'm still in the media.

But stranger things have happened, I guess. After all, the "Same Old Steelers" really did become four-time Super Bowl champions, didn't we?

—TERRY BRADSHAW

PREFACE

THE *BETTER THAN LIFTING THINGS* TITLE OF THIS BOOK IS IN honor of legendary sports columnist Red Smith, who finished his career with the *New York Times*, passing in 1982 at age 76.

While I'm not certain enough people outside of the newspaper business remember this gentle, wonderful man who won a Pulitzer Prize with the *Times*, perhaps this reminder will familiarize him with a few more.

In Jerome Holtzman's 1973 book, *No Cheering in the Press Box*, Red Smith described his profession as being, well, "a lot better than lifting things."

Simply and clearly said. That was Red Smith.

True enough, the heaviest thing Red had to lift was his typewriter or a piece of luggage. He loved the business of sportswriting, not so much the weighty burden of the writing process, but he lived for the people he met, the events he observed, and the thrill of being there.

I was extremely fortunate to have met Red a few times. The first occasion was in the press lounge at Three Rivers Stadium in 1974, when I was in my mid-20s, working for the *Pittsburgh Press*. I approached him, a bit nervously, and told him how honored I was to meet him.

"God bless you, son," Red said, smiling warmly.

I would see him at Super Bowls and other big games throughout the next several years, usually just exchanging hellos and smiles. The last time I remember speaking to Red was at the NFC Championship Game between the Philadelphia Eagles and the Dallas Cowboys, Jan

11, 1981, in freezing Veterans Stadium. On a single-digit day with 30 mph winds, Red was seated in that dreadfully drafty press box next to the *Times'* NFL writer, Bill Wallace.

I remember that Red was shivering with a cold and his usually ruddy complexion had taken on a bluish tint. I wondered why a 75-year-old man in such wretched conditions would still want to watch men play games and write about them. But that was Red Smith, who always cherished not having to lift things for a living and considered the writing, while it made him sweat and bleed, a reasonable tradeoff for the joy of being there.

I think back now to a literal example of Red's words. Working a summer job at the Seltzer's Lebanon Bologna Company in Palmyra, Pa., during college, I was stationed for a while across the meat-packing assembly line with a man named Tom. His daily task was to grab one cold, metal handle of a 100-pound tub of meat while the guy across from him grabbed the other. For a month or so, together we dumped the heavy tub into a grinder.

Tom said he did this for 27 years, and all that ever changed was the size of his forearms and the guy across from him.

Indeed, every time I concluded a summer job and went back to college to prepare for what I hoped would be my newspaper career, I thought about how fortunate I was that physical labor occupations were only mine for a couple of months.

Yes, during our sportswriting careers most of us regularly complained about long hours and short-sighted editors, but, in the end, reporting on and writing about sports for a newspaper was, without a doubt, "a lot better than lifting things."

Thanks for the reminder, Red.

INTRODUCTION

E VER SINCE I LEFT THE NEWSPAPER BUSINESS, PEOPLE HAVE BEEN telling me that I need to write a book.

OK, yeah, maybe, I would always say.

More than they realized, book writing is hard work, and I never comprehended how so many of my colleagues could labor over books before or after their daily newspaper drudgery.

I still can't fathom how my old colleague, the iconic Furman Bisher, who worked this profession for so long that he once actually scored an interview with Shoeless Joe Jackson, could grind out a dozen books while also writing a daily column for more than 60 years.

Hell, after I finished writing my daily stories at a Super Bowl or a U.S. Open, all I wanted was a burger and a few beers—no more writing, for God's sake. I'd rather stick a repair tool in my eye.

Thankfully, though, I finally did get to this book after all, on my own time, in between doctor appointments, selling our house in Atlanta, moving to Florida, seeing our four grandkids (Tyler and Bryan in Orlando; Luke and Lucy in Dallas) as much as possible and making an occasional visit to what used to be my golf game.

I've started to write this book several times in recent years, only to be thwarted temporarily for various reasons. Some were personal, but some were bold-headline-worthy developments you never could have predicted.

For instance, Joe Paterno and Tiger Woods—two huge figures in my career—were always going to be key chapters, and the dramatic changes to their stories demanded some major rewriting.

My old friend, John Madden, died in 2021, necessitating some editing to his chapter.

For those of you who were familiar with my career and might have lost track of me in recent years, I left the *Atlanta Journal-Constitution* in 2005 after 26 years, covering mostly the NFL and golf, and took a position with The Golf Club of Georgia in Alpharetta, Ga., sensing (correctly, it turns out) that newspapers were declining at an alarming pace.

The Golf Club of Georgia, though financially shaky for much of its member-owned existence, was a fresh, fun place to work for a few years following my exit from the *AJC*. My old friend Jeff Paton, the club's Director of Golf, basically invented a position for me (Director of Business Development), and it became very exciting, rewarding work. (The pleasure portion was OK, too, with playing privileges at a 36-hole club I never could have afforded to join).

We conducted our annual Georgia Cup Match between the U.S. Amateur and British Amateur Champions the week before the Masters and then in 2006 established the United States Collegiate Championship, which became the premier college golf event in the country.

Unfortunately, the good times didn't last. Three years into the job, our membership director was fired, and I agreed to add those duties to my PR role. More earning power, but also more pressure, something I was trying to reduce from my life after newspapers.

Then, in 2013, the club went into foreclosure and soon plummeted even further into decline. Beating out ClubCorp (my preference) with an all-cash offer, Horseshoe Bend Country Club owner Ben Kenny purchased The Golf Club of Georgia and changed nearly everything about the place we knew and loved.

Predictably, he deemed me identifiable with the previous regime and abruptly changed my status from "employed" to "unrestricted free agent."

Six months later, after dabbling in my own consulting and communication business with a partner who was, as it turns out, lousy at communicating, I took the Membership Director job at my former competition, Hawks Ridge Golf Club in Ball Ground, Ga., and for 2 ½ years enjoyed great satisfaction stealing some members from GCOG and the aforementioned Kenny.

I will always be grateful to my old friend Frank Tobin for connecting me with Hawks Ridge owners Joe Jillson and Mike Nixon, who gave me the opportunity to complete some unfinished business after the ordeal at GCOG and help their club a little bit in the process.

Thanks also to Hawks Ridge members like John Smoltz, Heath Slocum, and Bob Bird, who welcomed me warmly at a time when my pride needed some repairs, and both GM Jennifer Oliff and Phil Sheridan in the Men's Grill.

From those good times at The Golf Club of Georgia, my thanks to Lindsay Caye, Denise Gibby, Jeff Paton, Randy Waldron, and the late Bill Fralic, who helped the newspaper guy pull off a second career.

Thanks also to Terry Nau, my old pal and newspaper colleague at Penn State and State College, who in the spring of 2020 asked me to write a chapter for his book about my year at the *Pennsylvania Mirror* in 1973-74, stirring the creative juices that finally got me to finish mine.

Thanks to my former *AJC* colleague, Dave Kindred, the finest sports columnist in America, for his advice and encouragement in the book's final stages. And to my old friend from Hershey, Jim Reed, who reconnected me with our Hershey Country Club mentor, Jay Weitzel.

Special thanks, of course, to my wonderful wife, Nora, who remains my biggest fan and encouraged me to stay with this book project, along with my fabulous daughters, Jessica and Katie, and my cousin, Doug Sheeley, with whom I reunited in 2012 after almost 40 years.

No, they said, it hasn't been too long since you left the newspaper business.

Yes, they said, people still remember you from both Pittsburgh (I was with the old *Pittsburgh Press* for five years, mostly covering the Steelers in their glory years) and the *AJC,* where I was on the scene for 20 Masters, eight British Opens, 12 U.S. Opens, most of my 17 Super Bowls and hundreds of other NFL games.

And, yes, they insisted, the stories and anecdotes about sports people they love still hold up.

I think they do, too, and I hope you enjoy them.

Some were never sufficiently PG-rated for a newspaper. Some just were not what a daily beat writer or columnist could work into a limited space.

Some just weren't ready to be told.

A few of them you might have heard, but most of them you have not.

Despite some troubling times with the *AJC*—dating back to the merger of the *Journal and Constitution* in the early 1980s and the devastating death of my pal and golf writer Tom McCollister in 1999—overall I was very lucky as a sportswriter, which I decided on as a profession in 9th grade, inspired by reading Jim Murray's syndicated column in my local paper.

At Penn State, where the *Daily Collegian* was published five days a week and served as invaluable experience for writing professionally (not to mention, probably saving my journalism degree), I was there for the Nittany Lions' 31-game unbeaten streak that ended in 1970, working next to veteran beat writers such as Bill Lyon and Sandy Padwe of the *Philadelphia Inquirer,* Frank Bilovsky of the *Philadelphia*

Bulletin and Bill Heufelder of the *Pittsburgh Press*. They treated me as a peer, not a student journalist, and I always will be grateful for their kindness and camaraderie.

A little more than a year after graduation, after Terry Nau allowed me a wild and wonderful 11 months at the *Pennsylvania Mirror* in State College, Pa., I took a job at the *Pittsburgh Press*, where I eventually became the youngest beat writer in the NFL (at 25), covering the Steelers of the '70s—the greatest team of all-time—and the greatest owners ever, the Rooneys.

Sincere thanks to Terry Bradshaw for agreeing to write the foreword to this book. I have truly valued his friendship from the mid-1970s, when he helped a young reporter handle the giant task of covering such an iconic team, to recent years, when we finally reconnected during the fourth quarter of our lives.

Thanks always to Bill Heufelder, Sandy Padwe, and long-time NFL executive Ernie Accorsi, a fellow Hershey, Pa., native, who were largely responsible for my landing the *Pittsburgh Press* job. They were confident I could write myself off the desk, and they were right, and it became the turning point of my newspaper career.

In 1979 I moved to the *Atlanta Journal-Constitution*, to cover the Falcons and the NFL, securing a year-round writing position that was an upgrade from the *Press,* where even beat writers had to work the desk for a couple of months in their "off-season". But I never stopped missing the people and energy of Pittsburgh and almost went back a couple of years later to take a columnist job at the *Post-Gazette*.

At the *AJC* in 1994, quite luckily, I was asked to cover my true passion when I landed the golf beat, and guess who appeared? Tiger Woods, of course, and I was there for 10 of his major wins.

Pretty damn good trifecta—Penn State, the Steelers, and Tiger— and I've never taken for granted my good fortune.

The same for being surrounded by great writers. In Pittsburgh, the best guys were Phil Musick and Roy McHugh. In Atlanta, the heavyweights were Kindred and Furman Bisher.

Few of us got rich as sports writers—we all worked too many weekends, missed too many holidays, and often injured our marriages—but we were on the scene for many of the biggest moments in sports history.

Like one of my idols, the late Red Smith, I always first considered myself a newspaper reporter, rather than a sportswriter or a sports columnist. Report the news accurately and fairly and try to entertain people a bit in the process. That was always the goal during my entire newspaper career, and it even carried over when I shifted to public relations and membership sales. I never lied about a product or promised anything I couldn't deliver.

Tom McCollister, my old friend and mentor at the *AJC*, valued fairness more than anything else, with the goal to look his story subject comfortably in the eye the following day.

That goal barely exists in today's world, but it should.

I hope you enjoy the book.

—GLENN SHEELEY
(January 2024)

BETTER THAN LIFTING THINGS

CHAPTER 1

COVERING GOLF vs. ANYTHING ELSE

W HEN FRIENDS OF MINE HAVE ASKED ME FOR MANY YEARS about covering golf and football for a living, curious to know which I liked best, this is the first thing I always say:

"Well, let me put it this way. I covered NFL football for 20 years, and not once after we got done writing did we go play football."

Covering golf, especially if you love it, is the gravy sports beat of any newspaper or magazine. Once you have covered golf, especially PGA Tour golf, you can't cover anything else. It's that simple.

You're often in Florida, California, or Arizona, so it's usually warm.

Nobody hits you with a jock strap or sweat sock in the middle of a locker room.

You can't play golf after dark, so there is a limit to how long it is going to take, unlike, say, a U.S. Open tennis match going past midnight or a four-OT NBA game.

Beyond that, the athletes aren't usually naked and cursing, which is standard operating procedure in the NFL.

1

(Then again, I do remember Greg Norman after one of his late Augusta swoons, almost naked in bikini-cut briefs, posing the question when I suggested that eventually, he'll win a green jacket, "How much fucking later is it going to be?")

Any time I wanted to complain about covering golf, all I had to do was think of Soldier Field in January, when my mustache once froze, or the infamous 59-below Bengals-Chargers playoff game on Jan. 10, 1982, in Cincinnati. It was 13-below zero as I awoke that morning and ice had formed on the INSIDE of my hotel window.

As I mentioned, if you loved golf as I did, then covering it was the best thing that could happen to you as a sportswriter.

Now it wasn't extremely common to hit the golf course after we were done with covering a particular tournament that day, but we sure enough did it occasionally—especially in Europe, where that lovely 5-hour time difference is the best thing since the Pro-V1 offered up both distance and softness. If you didn't mind a long day, you could play early in the morning and finish up before your Eastern Time zone boss even got out of bed.

On one occasion in Scotland, I got through playing 18 holes, grabbed a pay phone in the clubhouse bar, and called into an 8 a.m. Saturday morning golf show in Atlanta.

When the Open was at Royal Lytham in England in 2001 (the year David Duval won), I filed my first story for the day, a Sergio Garcia feature, at 5:30 p.m. local time, then went down the road with some buddies to play Blackpool Golf Club, enjoying the UK's extensive daylight hours. Playing surprisingly well, I shot 75, drove back to Lytham, showered, returned to the media center, wrote a second story, and filed it by 7:30 p.m. Eastern time.

You gotta love it. It sure beat a Browns-Steelers game off Lake Erie in December.

Don't get me wrong, we worked hard—sometimes I wrote four stories a day at the majors, and we could easily put in a 16-hour day at a U.S. Open, where the deadlines always were tighter than a USGA fairway—but we savored the perks, too.

We were very fortunate to have played some of the world's best courses, especially the Monday after the tournament concluded, and we seldom had to go into our pockets for greens fees. I always liked to say that the best five words in golf were, "You're all taken care of." (Ok, six words, if you break up the contraction.)

Conversely, the worst five words you could hear were, "Will you be paying separately?"

Wait…what?

Free golf was basically an accepted perk of the golf writing business. Did we tell our bosses we were accepting it? No, not usually, but we never felt it was compromising our ability to work the tournament, and nobody really cared if you were doing your job well. Plus, the easy way around that problem was to merely take your boss to play one day at, say, the Atlanta Athletic Club or East Lake, and get him comped also. End of issue.

Sometimes we paid, for instance, in Scotland, where you could play a local high-quality public links course for 15 pounds or so, right next to Royal Troon.

Or maybe at Pinehurst, where there are so many great Donald Ross courses in the area that you could play for 25 bucks and get nearly the same quality as you could at the resort.

One Ross course there even offered an afternoon rate of $20 that included a free cover charge at the local gentlemen's club.

Does life get any better than this?

At the British Open, U.S. Open, or PGA Championship, often we were able to play the tournament course on Monday, and usually from the Sunday hole locations, too. It enabled me to play some of the world's greatest courses, like St. Andrews, Carnoustie, Whistling Straits, Shinnecock, Pinehurst No. 2, Riviera, Pebble Beach, Oak Hill, Medinah and Augusta National. Sometimes I'd write a story about the experience, which I did for St. Andrews and Augusta.

You can't put Augusta in the same Monday-after category as the other majors because it's still a very limited opportunity. I'm not sure how it is now, but when I was covering golf for the *Atlanta Journal-Constitution,* you would be placed in a lottery to play the Monday after the Masters once every seven years. I played Augusta National the day after the 1999 Masters and was a year away from being able to play again when I left the paper in 2005. (It wasn't going to keep me from leaving, but I must admit, I thought about it.)

The hardest thing about playing Augusta for the first time is trying to remain calm. It also doesn't help when you're playing into a three-club wind, aren't allowed to hit range balls, and must wait an hour and 15 minutes on the 10TH tee, the start of Amen Corner, to begin your round.

When I finally got over the ball, I had been swinging one of those weighted clubs for so long, my regular driver felt like a toy club and I snap-hooked my tee shot on the 10th into the left trees. I managed to make bogey, two putting from the front of the green, but ran into trouble at the difficult 11th.

My tee shot settled in the right rough, where during a rainy week the gallery had turned it into a crusty, muddy mess. My second, a 6-iron, flared right and smacked into the back of a guy hitting off the 12th tee.

Turns out it was a scoring official from Europe, who was OK, but I ended up just right of the green, from where I was lucky to make a bogey. I mentioned that to my Augusta National caddie, who said, "I don't know, if you had hit him in the head, I think you would have been on the green."

There were a couple of other highlights. I got up-and-down for par from the back bunker at No. 12, which any number of tour players would have cherished. I also birdied the par-5 8th, the ball hitting the back of the cup, popping into the air, and returning to the hole.

I shot 91 with only a trio of three-putts, from the Sunday pins, and wasn't all that disappointed, having driven the ball dreadfully and managing to find Rae's Creek twice on the par-5 13th.

I vowed to return in the future and try to do it all more sanely— have lunch, spend some time on the range and putting green, and enjoy a leisurely round.

Alas, it never happened, and probably will not now, being a retired Florida resident. But one experience at that hallowed place was plenty special, and all it cost me was a $90 caddie fee.

St. Andrews was equally interesting. Though it's not usually hard to get on the Old Course, which is public and runs right through the town, during Open Week it can be a challenge.

I was very lucky to have been hosted by Grant Spaeth, the former USGA president, and was joined that day by Mark Soltau, then of the *San Francisco Chronicle*, who carried a legit 2-handicap. Birdieing the Road Hole and shooting a 1-under 71 pretty much proved it.

I didn't do as well on the famed 17th, to say the least. The Old Course Hotel, as it turns out, is a lot closer to you than it appears on TV and not as far to the right as you would expect. So, when I came out of my tee shot a bit, it flared right and smacked into the side of the old building on the way to a triple-bogey seven. My caddie had seen the hotel plunked many times and barely reacted. I, meanwhile, was worried my ball would cause the hotel facade to start crumbling and provoke an international incident.

I ended up shooting an 86, which was rather mediocre in that we were playing from the shorter yellow tees, but I did manage to eagle the short, par-4 9th, chipping in from just off the front of the green.

At the round's conclusion, Grant enabled us to stow our clubs in the Royal & Ancient Clubhouse, which was pretty cool. We wandered up the street for a couple of pints and a burger, talking to a few townsfolk who had watched us finish our round, which is the unique aspect of playing the Old Course in the middle of a Scottish Village.

At the 1998 Pebble Beach AT&T tournament, we were playing the fabled course on the Monday after—myself, Doug Ferguson of the *Associated Press*, Jim McCabe of the *Boston Globe*, and Cliff Brown of the *New York Times*. A few of my favorite guys, most definitely, with Fergie by far the best of the foursome. He even still carries a 1-iron and produces these low, bullet tee shots that run out forever.

We had a 10:47 a.m. tee time, which we knew would be dicey for finishing the round because California days in January are famous for their stingy daylight. So, because I was up early and very excited, I called over to the Pro Shop and asked if we could possibly tee off a bit earlier to guarantee finishing the round.

Without any hesitation, he said, "No, that's why it's free."

British Open Mondays were sometimes tough to negotiate for the media. Some of these old clubs were intent on giving the course back to their members immediately Monday morning, having shut them off for several weeks during tournament preparations, and a bunch of Yank golf writers weren't about to take up their tee times.

So, as a result, after the 1999 Open Championship at Carnoustie, we played the Old Course at St. Andrews. And on the Monday after St. Andrews, we went over to play Carnoustie. The club was happy to accommodate U.S. writers after the horrendous publicity following the Open the year before, when the controversial rough just off the fairway was ridiculous at a foot high. (Jean van de Velde could have hidden in there, and probably should have).

We played Riviera after the 1995 PGA and saw O.J.'s old locker in the clubhouse.

We played the just-opened Whistling Straits the Monday after the 1998 Women's Open at adjacent Blackwolf Run, and it took three hours just to play nine holes, with four caddies in a blustering wind.

We played Winged Foot the Monday after the 1997 PGA, with Davis Love's rainbow clearly of no use to our group. Four of us, with caddies, hit off the first tee, and only one guy found his ball in that dreadful rough.

We played Shinnecock the Monday after the 2004 U.S. Open, when the course was so rock hard in the final round, nobody could keep it on the 7th green. (Three of our guys did on Monday, but only because it was watered heavily the night before).

We played Oak Hill the Monday after the 1995 Ryder Cup and I had to quit after the 13th hole to make a plane. It was the hardest golf course I had ever played, and I was fine with leaving 7-inch long, half-inch wide bluegrass rough that was almost unplayable. Even the late Tim Rosaforte, my talented playing partner, thought so, and he had Popeye-type forearms back then.

We played England's Royal Birkdale that Monday after the 1998 British Open, and a few holes into it after a tee shot, I collapsed on the ground, holding my right side, where I had undergone kidney cancer surgery in March. Scar tissue had broken loose, and it felt like a knife sticking in my side.

Rosaforte, his fellow *Golf World* pal, John Hawkins, and Jeff Babineau of the *Orlando Sentinel* were with me that day and felt bad that I had to stop playing. I walked the rest of the front nine, just carrying a wedge and hitting a couple of chips while they played on. Pretty soon, out of nowhere, it went from mild and sunny to cool, windy, and raining sideways. In other words, typical British Isles weather.

"I've got my excuse," I told Rosie, Hawk, and Babs, heading for the parking lot. "How about you guys?"

The 1994 U.S. Senior Open at Pinehurst was one of the most enjoyable tournaments I ever covered, and it was one of my first majors, having taken over the golf beat at the *AJC* that year. We stayed at the famous Pinehurst resort, ate lunch every day at the hotel buffet, and enjoyed tee times set up for us all week by the wonderful Melody Dossenbach of the Pinehurst PR staff. She was so accommodating that when I told her after five straight rounds that I couldn't play on Saturday morning because my wife was arriving then from Atlanta, she seemed almost insulted!

It was a great week and about to get even better. Melody had set up me, Jaime Diaz of *Sports Illustrated*, Dave LaGarde of the *New Orleans Times-Picayune*, and Ron Green Jr. of the *Charlotte Observer* to play Pinehurst No. 2 Monday at 10 a.m.

The trouble was, back then the USGA still used an 18-hole Monday playoff to decide the champion in the event of a tie after 72 holes, and things were looking rather bleak. (At least for Monday media golf, anyway.) Fortunately, South Africa's colorful and sometimes crazy Simon Hobday saved the day at the 18th.

Hobday happily watched Jim Albus miss a tying birdie attempt, followed by Graham Marsh conveniently leaving his par putt on the lip. After lagging his 40-foot birdie putt to about three feet, Hobday sank the victory-clinching putt, then let go of his putter as though too hot to handle. He fell to his knees and kissed the grass.

The next time I saw Hobday out on Tour, I congratulated him on his Senior Open victory.

"Greatest putt I've ever seen," I told him.

Taken aback, Hobday said, "What? Are you daft, lad? It was only a few feet."

"Maybe so," I said. "But if you miss it, you're playing Graham Marsh on Pinehurst No. 2 in a playoff the next morning. But you make it and we're playing No. 2 at 10 a.m."

"Ah, I get it, lad," Hobday said, grinning. "You're welcome."

CHAPTER 2

PENN STATE

MY DECISION TO ATTEND PENN STATE IN 1969 COULD NOT have worked out better. The University Park main campus was huge—sometimes a half-hour walk to classes from my dorm— and was famous for its harsh winters, but the rewards were plentiful.

Most importantly, I wrote for the *Daily Collegian*, the student newspaper, for four years and probably received 10 times the useful experience that a journalism degree could provide. (Nothing against my journalism professors, who were mostly wonderful, but there's no better way to learn to be a journalist than by being one, and with such a quality student newspaper at Penn State, that's what we were able to do.)

The *Collegian* had a legitimate 30,000 circulation back then and was published five days a week. We covered national stories, even occasionally breaking them, and I worked at least 40 hours a week there—even more during football season. I progressed from a freshman reporter just trying to get a byline to serving as Sports Editor in my senior year.

I would encourage anybody who wants to write for a living to do the same. You might feel like you are ignoring your classes—and, of course, you are—but if you want to work for a newspaper (if they still exist), this is where you get the foundation.

Having a permanent national story to follow such as Joe Paterno and Penn State football certainly helped the profile—I was there with Jack Ham, Mike Reid, Lydell Mitchell, Franco Harris, and PSU's 31-game unbeaten streak—but there were many great experiences all along the way, even with the lesser sports.

One of my favorite stories came from one of the most obscure sports—fencing, of all things—which *Collegian* sports editor Don McKee asked me to cover during my freshman year. I jumped at the opportunity, hoping it might allow me a regular byline in the paper.

Since I knew nothing about the sport, I decided to take a fencing class during the next term for research. Little did I know that the instructor, Coach Dick Klima, was world-renowned, had studied the sport in France and coached in the Olympics, and possessed an ego roughly the size of Beaver Stadium.

The first day Coach Klima passed out foils, masks, and bibs and gave us a few basic lunges, parries, and strategies to work on. After we "fenced" for 10 or 15 minutes, he motioned for us to huddle up near him.

Then he said, dead seriously, "Now I'm going to divide you into two groups—fencers and spastics."

I was trying not to laugh at how cold that sounded when he continued, "Now I don't want any of you spastics to feel dismayed. I've seen some spastics get as high as a B."

Equally cold, but also hilarious.

Fortunately, I was placed in the fencers group, possibly, I'm thinking, because he heard I'll be covering his team and perhaps appreciated my attempt at familiarization.

A couple of sessions into it, we started flailing away at the opening of the class period, and he called for us to huddle up.

He mentioned a particular lunge-parry move that he had introduced to us previously, and demanded, looking at me, "Mr. Sheeley, demonstrate!"

Stunned, I approached him and performed the move.

"Mr. Sheeley," he said with zero hesitation, "over with the spastics!"

Both brutal and hysterical at the same time. Priceless.

I survived the class and covering his Nittany Lion fencers and eventually got some higher-profile assignments, like helping with football and basketball.

Penn State basketball was OK, but it never held the prestige of Penn State football, so naturally I was delighted to eventually get some opportunities to be around Paterno's team.

While I don't consider it particularly pleasant that I met the infamous Jerry Sandusky in that role and interviewed him many times, it was quite a kick covering such a prominent national story as Penn State football right in my backyard. Beyond that, it enabled me to meet the national writers from Pittsburgh, Philadelphia, or New York who were there every week, home or on the road, with the Nittany Lions.

Not only did Penn State beat writers like Bill Heufelder of the *Pittsburgh Press* or Sandy Padwe of the *Philadelphia Inquirer* become good friends who were valuable contacts, but they were even a source of some extra cash. Because the out-of-town writers were on such tight deadlines for Saturday games and the Penn State locker room was then located a mile or so from the stadium, at the Ice Rink, I started a gameday quotes service for them, usually for $10 each. I'd race down to the locker room for maybe 15 minutes, take a shuttle back to the stadium, type up a few paragraphs of quotes on one of those old 5-carbon paper sheets, and pass them out. Sometimes I got $50 for each home game, and that was big money for a college kid back then.

Hard as it is to fathom these days—my oldest daughter first flew at 11 months—I was 19 when I took my first jet airplane trip, the Penn State team charter from Harrisburg to Knoxville in 1972 for a Sept. 16 game with the Volunteers to open the season. Penn State ended up losing 28-21, but that wasn't my strongest memory from the trip.

When Bobby Majors of Tennessee fielded the ball for his first punt return, I quickly discovered that Northeast journalism was significantly different than what regularly occurred in the South.

"Go, Bobby, Go! Go, Bobby, Go!" the local writers screamed, standing at their seats.

I was stunned. So much for the journalistic credo, "No cheering in the press box." Sadly, they were following something different in Big Orange Country.

I was on a Penn State charter to Champaign, Ill., in 1972 when the pilot attempted to land the jet in a 40-mph crosswind. The nose hit, the plane swerved wildly at nearly a 45-degree angle, then straightened violently. I remember looking over at gigantic defensive linemen clutching armrests like hands on a roller coaster bar. Scary as it was, the scene pretty much wrote my lead for me. With Penn State still suffering from turnover problems in a 35-17 loss to Illinois, I wrote in my freelance story for the *Philadelphia Daily News*, "the pilot almost turned over the plane."

I was extremely excited to be writing for the *Daily News,* but the assignment met a huge obstacle. Several of us were sickened by some airline sandwiches that were brought from the plane to the PSU media suite and I spent much of the game in the press box men's room, peering now and then from a small window.

I was able to file the story a day later, thankfully, because the *Daily News* had no Sunday paper. By then, I had written a story I was very proud of, for a paper I read every day and one that employed some of my favorite writers. When the paper came out that Monday afternoon, I bought a few copies and headed to the Roy Rogers restaurant on College Ave., to check out my story in the *Daily News* over a couple of burgers. I must have read it 20 times, still in minor disbelief that I was looking at my byline in a Philly paper—not to mention getting paid for it! I think I got $75, and that was more than my monthly rent for the single room I had that year.

If people who write for a newspaper ever try to claim that they don't get a kick out of seeing their byline in the paper, don't believe them. First time, every time. I experienced it thousands of times, and it never got old.

When I started covering Penn State football, a highlight was always the Friday night dinner which PSU Sports Information Director John Morris hosted for the writers covering the game. The *Collegian*, the *Centre Daily Times*, and the *Pennsylvania Mirror* writers were invited, too, though it was chiefly for the writers from Philly, Pittsburgh, or New York. Often the dinner was held at the Boalsburg Steak House, just down the road from State College.

One night I was sitting next to Bruce Keidan of the *Philadelphia Inquirer*, and he asked me what bar he should visit after dinner. I asked him if he had ever been to the My-Oh-My bar on College Ave. He had not, so I suggested that as a good place for some local flavor.

But be careful, I said. There is a front and a back entrance and there are two distinctly different types of people that typically use those specific doors. Come in the back door, I told him, and you're in the gay section of the bar. Enter through the front door and it's mostly redneck guys in wrestling windbreakers.

Interesting, he said, leaving the steak house.

As it turned out, he had no idea how interesting it would become. You see, I had intentionally reversed the doors and lifestyles, meaning if he entered through the front door, which was likely, he could have run directly into a guy dressed in a sailor hat and leather chaps.

Bruce never talked about it Saturday at the game, so I guess we'll never know.

While Penn State sports and the newspaper were my main focus, it wasn't all fun and games.

In the spring of 1970, huge protests erupted at the university after President Nixon's invasion of Cambodia and the Kent State shootings. Things were so bad that our spring term was suspended, allowing students to be sent home with pass/fail grades. (Great, if you were barely passing a course, which was the case with me and my German class.)

A few days before, I was leaving the *Collegian* office one night when I noticed a ruckus at Old Main, the administration building. Pretty soon, dozens of National Guardsmen in riot gear were encircling the area and I almost got caught on the wrong side of the perimeter. I sprinted to my car and felt fortunate to get out of there unscathed.

In the spring of 1973, when the Watergate hearings were the biggest story on the globe, I was watching the proceedings in my room on TV one day, when I had to pull myself away to attend class for one of my easier electives, "Courtship & Marriage." One day a week, a graduate assistant conducted the class and usually held it outside. On this day, unbelievably, we were sitting on the grass near Old Main, passing around contraceptive devices. True story.

Frustrated that I had to leave the hearings for this, I said to the grad assistant, "This class is interrupting my education."

Fortunately, I was taking the class pass/fail, or that crack likely would have cost me a couple of grades.

Because I spent so much time at the newspaper office or covering events, attending classes was fairly low on my priority list, and with that decision came a few issues.

Like forgetting about my midterm exam in Psychology 13.

The course was Child Psychology and was conducted totally by TV, with the professor speaking from his office on videotape.

Hoping to avoid a failing grade for missing the exam, I called the prof and claimed that I had been ill, and asked if I could take the test at another time.

"Which period does your class meet?" he asked.

"Fourth period," I said.

"Well," he said, "do you know which class period is meeting right now?"

Yikes. Oops. Never mind.

After claiming to attend his class regularly, without thinking I had called him during the class period.

I hung up, relieved that I had not given my name.

Things like this happen, of course, when you spend 50 hours at the *Collegian* every week and maybe five hours with your classes.

But it was worth it. Despite these academic setbacks, I managed to get both my journalism degree and my newspaper experience.

And some other experiences, too.

In the spring of 1973, my senior year, my Philly pal Steph Rosenfeld (who would serve as best man at my first wedding), oversaw Penn State's Colloquy speaker's program and had lined up an impressive group—comedian George Carlin, consumer advocate Ralph Nader and my writing idol, Rod Serling of *Twilight Zone* fame.

(Steph always called me "Sport" as a reference to my sportswriting and was one of my biggest fans. The feeling was mutual, as Steph would eventually enjoy an incredible career as a TV news producer, political PR, and communications expert, and finally as an authority on strategic-risk communications. In other words, he did the serious stuff, and I was still watching and writing about games.)

Anyway, a couple of hours before, this being a typical Penn State Friday afternoon, a friend of mine, Rhonda Blank, and I were having Happy Hour beers on College Ave. By the time we got to Rec Hall for the Colloquy program, we were both rolling and ready for an entertaining night. For me, that meant listening to anything Serling had to say, enjoying Carlin's zany humor, and being fairly disinterested in what Nader professed about the dangers of driving a Corvair. Indeed, I had learned to drive on one and was still alive. Just saying.

Everyone was informed early on that the proceedings would start a little late because Carlin was detained. Knowing what we know now about Carlin, it seemed obvious that he was probably too high to perform at that point and required a return to earth. Good time to visit the restroom, I told Rhonda.

On the way there, I passed a small room where, of all things, Steph was chatting with Rod Serling, who was tiny and well-tanned, in advance of his appearance. I glanced over for a second, whereupon Steph motioned for me to come in and said, "Don't you want to meet Rod Serling?"

Obviously, this was a big kick for any young writer, and I excitedly extended a hand, said hello, then turned to leave.

AND THEN STEPH SAID, "HEY, SPORT, DON'T YOU WANT TO DO YOUR ROD SERLING IMPRESSION FOR ROD?"

What I experienced next was a confluence of mild excitement, shock, and sheer terror.

Although I thought some of my impersonations were pretty

good—I even did a Richard Nixon character for the campus radio station—I wasn't at the point where I felt comfortable doing one in front of my subject. ESPECIALLY ROD FREAKING SERLING!!!"

What I should have done was offer a "Yeah, right" and disappear, but for some reason (I'm guessing too many beers) I stood in front of the famous little man from California and started into the impersonation. This included doing the whole mouth and clenched teeth thing and emphasizing the familiar *Twilight Zone* intro, which spoke of "traveling through another dimension not only of sight and sound, but of mind."

After a slight pause, Rod Serling looked at me and said, "Oh, my God, do I sound that bad?"

It was at this point I allowed a forced laugh, waved goodbye, went back to my seat, and informed Rhonda Blank that "my life is pretty much over now."

Decades later Steph and I can laugh about it, but in 1973 it took me a while to get over it. Many years later, when the rage was putting famous voices on your answering machine, I had recovered enough to honor Rod with this one to amuse my friends:

"BEEP… "You're entering a dimension known as Glenn's phone. Please leave your message at the tone."

What saved my journalism degree at Penn State? Mostly, it was working for *the Daily Collegian* in general and acquiring real-life newspaper experience before I even came close to graduating. My professors read me in the paper regularly—much more regularly than they saw me in class.

Another bit of assistance came through the satirical issue we published in the spring of 1973, the traditional time for the sports editor to step aside and promote his assistant sports editor. Mine was Ray McAllister, who went on to become a successful author.

We did a takeoff on Paterno's decision in January of 1973 to turn down a multi-million dollar offer (which was huge back then) from the NFL's New England Patriots. Centered around my decision to take a job in Cocoa, Fla., for the Brevard County edition of the *Orlando Sentinel-Star*, the story was headlined, "Sheeley leaves Penn State for the Money" and took up most of the front page. We even ran an actual Penn State wrestling story across the top of the page to add some realism to the production.

I heard Paterno even got a good chuckle out of it, though he never admitted as much to me.

My good friend Terry Nau, the most prolific writer I ever met, was the *Collegian* sports editor before me. We traveled all around the northeast, covering Penn State football games, occasionally flying to the faraway ones, and partying as hard as we worked.

They were crazy, exciting times and I owe Terry immensely for my college newspaper experience and then later when we worked together for a year at the *Pennsylvania Mirror* in State College. He saved me from the disastrous move to Florida, which lasted barely over three months, taking me on at the *Mirror* in the fall of 1973, where I discovered that returning to work in your college town with a bit of cash in your pocket is about as good as it gets. Those 11 months with the *Mirror* were the best time of my professional life and I think all of us who worked there would say the same thing.

But even when we were at the *Collegian,* occasionally Terry or I would break a national story.

One night I was drinking at one of my favorite haunts, The Lion's Den—where you could enter underaged with nothing more than a doctored driver's license—when a buddy of mine asked me to take over at the door TO CARD PEOPLE, of all things. This was one for the books, me being underaged and checking IDs. I even threw a guy out, laughing at, well, his doctored driver's license, of course.

Later in the evening, I ran into Steve Joachim, a star quarterback from Philadelphia who was still struggling for playing time with Joe Paterno. So much so, he said, before my semi-intoxicated eyes, that he was transferring to Temple.

In the morning, with a clearer head, I called Joachim back to confirm what he had told me in the bar. Indeed, it was true, and we managed to break the story in Tuesday's *Collegian*, from where it was picked up and distributed nationwide.

Not bad for a school newspaper we gave away for free.

CHAPTER 3

JOE PATERNO

THE JERRY SANDUSKY SCANDAL WAS TOUGH FOR ALL OF US WHO went to Penn State, especially the older PSU grads who were there when Penn State's football program was so dominating—and so image-perfect—in the late 1960s and early 1970s.

It was particularly difficult for those who knew Jerry Sandusky, interviewed him several times, and were so respectful of his boss, Joe Paterno.

Did I ever suspect anything of Sandusky, though I was just 19 or 20 as a student reporter at Penn State's *Daily Collegian*? No, I can't say that I did, but he always seemed a little, well, smarmy or goofy or whatever it was. Definitely not what you would expect of a guy who kept churning out tough, talented linebackers every year.

But, of course, the real issue is how the scandal affected the legacy of Joe Paterno.

I share the feeling with many others that Joe Paterno died of a broken heart. They can say it was lung cancer, but I think Joe died when Penn State's image died. It wasn't his firing, however unjustified, that killed him. It was the damage to everything he accomplished in his 61 years at Penn State. For a Board of Trustees interested only in damage control to destroy much of that legacy was criminal in itself.

Did Joe Paterno make mistakes handling (or not handling) the Sandusky situation? Who knows? I wasn't there, and it's not for me to say.

But one thing I do know is that nothing will diminish my respect for Joe Paterno, who had such a huge influence on me and so many others while at Penn State—and far beyond.

Let me tell you some things about Joe Paterno I will always cherish.

He always treated me, though just a beginning writer on the college paper, with the same respect he showed to the big-city guys from Pittsburgh, New York, or Philadelphia who covered his team. The *Collegian* reporters had earned absolutely zero credibility as we stood on his practice field and offered daily criticism of his team, but Joe gave us more respect than we deserved.

Heck, we even ran a mugshot of a turnover in the paper one day—a blurred football that prompted us to start calling him "Joe Paternover" when the 1970 team kept losing the football—and he still treated us like regular reporters, not the smart-assed kids we were.

When my father died at 52 of a heart attack in January of 1973, Joe and the Penn State athletic department sent flowers and a card to my little town of Palmyra, Pa. When I returned to campus for winter term that January, still numb from the tragedy, I stopped by Joe's office in Rec Hall to thank him for the gesture. Figuring he was too busy for more than a quick hello and an in-person expression of his condolences, Joe instead spent over an hour with me there, talking about his father and trying to soothe the pain of losing mine.

Mind you, this was only a week or so after he turned down the multi-million dollar offer to coach the New England Patriots of the NFL. In fact, that was the last thing my dad and I spoke about three days before he died, how he was proud of Joe for ignoring what was then huge cash and sticking with what he loved.

Joe remembered signing a copy of his book, *Football My Way*, for my dad a year before. It read: "To Mark, I hope you enjoy this as much as we have enjoyed having Glenn around here. Best wishes, Joe Paterno."

My dad showed it to everyone.

Did personal experiences form my opinion of Joe and make me less prone to criticize him for the Sandusky matter? Absolutely. I don't regret it or apologize for it. And I never will.

You give the benefit of the doubt to someone you so greatly respect. You just do.

My first conversation with Joe Paterno came in September of 1970.

You bet I was intimidated.

He was in his fifth year as head coach but had been there for 16 years as an assistant under Rip Engle. I was in my first year covering Penn State football as a student with *the Daily Collegian* and I was at practice that particular day, subbing for our sports editor, Dan Donovan.

As Paterno huddled with reporters after practice concluded, eventually I managed to spit out an awkward, stumbling question that had something to do with Penn State's game that week to open the season at Colorado. Joe, you had to realize, was accustomed to kid reporters throwing up on themselves the first time they appeared before those thick lenses.

When I finally stopped speaking, if you could call it that, I guess Joe presumed it was time then for him to say something.

What he said, after a few seconds of hesitation, was, "Where's Donovan?"

Friday night before a Penn State game typically brought us to a media gathering with Paterno at perhaps the home of Sports Information Director John Morris, the Boalsburg Steak House just down the road from State College, or perhaps Centre Hills Country Club. It consisted of writers from Pittsburgh, Philly, or New York who were in town for the game and usually a couple of locals.

One Friday night, Joe was speaking with a few reporters, who tried not to yawn, arguing that "Navy is awfully, awfully tough. We are going to have to play some great football to beat Navy. They're an awfully good football team."

"Joe, you're playing Army tomorrow."

"Oh, I mean, Army," said the coach.

People always assume all college football coaches are full of shit. This is basically true, but there are varying degrees. If on a BS/lying/deception scale of 1 to 10 Jackie Sherrill was, say, a 10, then Joe Paterno was probably a 1.

At those Friday night gatherings, I'm going to guess Joe Paterno was pretty unique. You see, something regularly happened there that in today's media world would have been unthinkable.

Simply put, Joe usually gave us his game plan, and sometimes in great detail. Seriously.

And here's the truly amazing part. Everybody agreed that it was off the record, uttered only to familiarize us during the game, and nobody ever wrote it.

Could a major college football coach do that today? Absolutely not, because somebody would have plastered it all over the internet in 10 minutes, thereby making it the last time a coach would elect to be so candid.

Was it journalistically proper for us to agree to it? Maybe so, maybe not. But a rare trust factor existed there that everyone just bought into. Not just the college reporters, but even the big-city writers who worked for the major metros.

A trust factor that is long gone.

Sadly, the same as Joe.

CHAPTER 4

THE BURGH

I LOVED PITTSBURGH WHEN I GOT THERE IN 1974 AND I STILL DO. I still get a stirring in my gut when thinking about all that was happening there in the '70s and my good fortune to be squarely in the middle of it.

While I've lived in the South for 44 years—in Georgia and now Florida—as a native of Hershey I'm a Pennsylvanian at heart. Ever since I moved to the western side of the state, I've never stopped missing the atmosphere and energy of Pittsburgh and the greatest sports fans anywhere.

It was my first time living in a big city and The Burgh was exactly what I needed. To have the Pirates, Steelers, and Penguins just outside my office door at the *Pittsburgh Press* was all a young journalist could want, especially at a time when newspapers counted almost as heavily as TV.

Yes, the Pittsburgh accent was a bit strange when first heard, but after a while, it became uniquely comforting. Live in Pittsburgh for a while and you can spot people born there as soon as they enter the conversation. The Pittsburgh people are Midwesterners more than they are Northeasterners like those on the Philly side of the state, and much friendlier.

I know a lot of cities try to claim their fans as the best in the land, but my vote goes to this group, which supported a God-awful NFL team for nearly 40 years before it became the best one that ever existed.

When I drove into town the first day, turning down the Blvd. of the Allies toward the Press building and spotting Three Rivers Stadium, I had no idea I would end up being the Steelers' beat guy just over a year later, but something told me this was going to be quite an adventure. Yes, the city was still dirty and smelly then, but it had great character and crazy characters. I would end up meeting and writing about many of them.

Like Billy Conn, the heavyweight boxer from Pittsburgh, who fought and lost to Joe Louis. We shared the same hangout, the old Forbes Street Inn in Squirrel Hill, where you could drink a scotch and water for $1.10.

Or Dave Pober, a rotund guy they called "Chopper," who wore bold polyester shirts that hugged his barrel of a belly. Dave knew everyone and spoke in short, staccato sentences. When he wasn't attending a sports event, he was a regular patron of the famous Primanti Brothers original restaurant in the Strip District, known for its giant sandwiches served on sharp crusted Italian bread, with everything on them, including French fries.

"I was in Primanti's yesterday," Chopper said one day at the bar of the Forbes Street Inn. "I ordered a shot of bourbon... there were French fries in it."

The Original Oyster House, established in 1870, was just a short walk from the Press Building and I stopped in there for lunch during those early days in town.

"Can I see a menu?" I said to a grizzled guy sucking on a Lucky.

"We gawt fish and we gawt oysters," he said. "We ain't gawt no fuckin' menus."

With that, he flicked his cigarette across the room, and it landed on the linoleum floor as a glowing bomb.

In that case, I said, "I'll have the fish sandwich, please."

When I came to the *Pittsburgh Press* in 1974, many of the Sports Department desks still had those old candlestick-style rotary phones with the separate piece to hold up to your ear. There were regular desk phones, too, but the old antique ones certainly added to the charm of the place. (When I left the *Press* in 1979, I tried to take along one of the old phones, which were being phased out, but I got caught by someone from Bell Telephone who claimed they were necessary for parts).

While the *Press* wasn't the best newspaper around, it sure had some talented people.

Like the quiet man, Roy McHugh, whose sensitive and smooth writing made him a Pittsburgh icon, first as Sports Editor, and then later as a city columnist. I never respected anyone in the business more than I did Roy. When he approached my desk and said, "Good column" in that unique whisper of a voice, that was all I ever needed to hear. My day was made. Heck, my month was made.

Or my old running buddy, Jeff Samuels, who was kind of a young Roy, just blooming into maturity as a writer, possessing that same gentle sensitivity. He was taken by cancer way too young, but I will always remember fondly our young days together at the *Press*, when we were thrilled to be in the middle of a frantic, big-city newsroom on a Saturday night, hitting the bars when it was all over and then grabbing a wee-hours meal at the Pancake Kitchen in Oakland.

We shared our dreams and goals and even hit some of them.

The same for Dan Donovan, whom I was also with at Penn State, having preceded me as sports editor at the *Collegian*. Working for one of the Pittsburgh papers was his lifetime goal and there he was, covering the Penguins. I was from the other side of the state and truthfully had envisioned Philadelphia as my place to start, but I was honored to be among these guys as they shared their wonderful town with me. Rather, their "tahn," as they say in The Burgh.

Clearly, Phil Musick was the writing star of Pittsburgh when I got there, and it was a title he deserved. He could make play-by-play writing on deadline damn near poetic. When you read his copy, even on morning deadlines, the words shot across the page with an unusual energy. When I was on the copy desk and handling his work, I hated cutting any of it, but Phil often wrote too long for his story's assigned space, and something had to go. As painful as it was for him to read a shortened version the next day, it was just as painful for me to have been forced to hold the knife. I would have gladly cut my own story instead.

A long-time Steelers beat man, Phil jumped to the *Post-Gazette* in 1976 for a columnist job, creating the NFL opening at the *Press* that I would eventually fill. His stay at the PG included some controversy when one of his columns showed an all-too-familiar likeness to something written by a prominent national columnist, but I never held that against Phil. He was an amazingly inventive writer, who absorbed gimmicks and phrases from other guys whom he loved to read and worked them into his own style. Sometimes he lost track of where he had read or heard something, or even if he indeed had created it. It was no different than a tale he would spin about once being in a particular city, meeting some girl, or dining at some restaurant. None of it probably existed, yet it was mostly harmless and always entertaining, nonetheless.

When Phil died in January 2010 at 71, it was a huge loss for the city of Pittsburgh. While we would regularly kid Phil about the BS he produced regarding on-the-road stories, absolutely no one denied his writing talent. He was the best in town, and it was an honor to be his partner on the beat in 1975.

At Super Bowl X against Dallas, we wrote 15 stories that night in Miami. I wrote eight and Phil wrote seven and I think we exhausted every word in our notebooks to describe how the once-lowly Steelers captured back-to-back Super Bowl wins with Chuck Noll's guidance, that incredible defense, and Terry Bradshaw's arm.

Working back at the hotel that night, we had two Big Macs each and shared a bottle of scotch, courtesy of a young lady named Tommie Lee Bill (I kid you not), whom we met early in the week at a Big Daddy Ed Roth's bar in Miami.

(Still single at the time, I won't bore you with the details, but as luck would have it, I had to share a room that week with Art Rooney's chauffeur, having been a late addition to the trip, and it created some, well, inconveniences.)

As much as I should probably avoid saying anything negative regarding our former *Press* sports editor, the late Pat Livingston, I am unable to resist. That Sunday night, as we were leaving the Super Bowl press box to begin our serious work back at the hotel, Livingston handed me three folded sheets of copy paper and told me to file it via telecopier back at the hotel. Yes, it was just his regular column, already written hastily in the press box. No more. Nothing special. Nothing extra because it was the Super Bowl. Just his typical shallow, silly stuff, completed quickly so he could get to the team party and dive into a few cocktails. I heard he got there before the players even showed up.

During that week in Miami, Livingston also demanded that our telecopier, a bulky, heavy facsimile machine in a suitcase that we used to send our stories back then, be kept in his room for his convenience.

So even though I had to schlep it through two airports, Phil and I had to visit Pat's room to use it.

While there wasn't much I could do about it, since Pat officially was "Sports Editor" and the main columnist, I managed some satisfying revenge. Every time I went to Pat's room, which I think was six times during the week, I also hit the $5.95 pay-per-view button on his TV.

When we checked out of the hotel on Monday morning, I happened to overhear Pat arguing with the hotel front desk person.

"This is an outrage!" he bellowed. "I didn't watch one goddam movie this week, let alone six!"

Bill Heufelder, who will love that story, was one of the finest writers I ever knew in the newspaper business. Indeed, he probably was too talented for newspapers. He had a novelist's touch and gentle personality—both seldom seen in those writing for daily consumption. At the *Press*, I would have put only Heufy and Roy McHugh in that category. Not surprisingly, they were great friends.

While most newspaper guys were okay with merely banging out stories as quickly as possible, Heufy crafted every sentence, taking full advantage of an afternoon newspaper's late deadline. After, say, a late Penguins or Duquesne basketball game, you might look over and see Heufy nodding off at his typewriter for a few minutes, only to suddenly reawaken and resume the same paragraph with no break in his sentence structure.

It was something to see.

Heufy also got me started in Pittsburgh with a furniture friend, when I had nothing more than what would fit in my old AMC Hornet. Bill and his wife gave me an old dinette table for my kitchen and organized a great deal through a friend for a couch, end table, bed, and nightstand, saving me from an early life of lying on my nasty carpet to watch TV or eat dinner.

Heufy and I hit it off from the start, dating back to the early '70s, when Bill also had the Penn State football beat and I was covering for the student newspaper, dreaming of doing it for a living.

Bob Smizik was clearly the best reporter on the *Press* sports staff and a tireless man on the Pirates beat, which is a wonderful existence if you live and breathe baseball, but it's a grueling one for travel and hours consumed. Indeed, baseball writers back then, more than any other beat writers, tended to be either single or divorced.

As a beat writer, Smizik was tougher than a cheap steak yet respected by the players because of his honesty and integrity. Smiz was also a great friend and colleague who introduced me to loads of people around town and took me to cool events that were just like him— Pittsburgh to the core.

We were walking down Market Street downtown one night and I happened to glance over at a bar, only to see the famous jazz group, The Ramsey Lewis Trio, playing with the club's doors open in the evening summer air.

"Is that The Ramsey Lewis Trio?" I asked Smiz.

"Yeah, I think so," he said. "Why?"

That was Pittsburgh in the 1970s. A Mister Rogers sighting would have been far more reason to gawk.

Smiz and I watched a closed-circuit telecast of the Ali-Foreman fight in Zaire on Oct. 30, 1974, at Pittsburgh's Syria Mosque. The picture was black-and-white and fuzzy. The screen looked like a white bed sheet. Quite a difference from today's global events broadcast in high-definition.

I'd often sit to the left of Smiz in the press box to just watch the Pirates game, either in my free time or before heading into the office for my graveyard desk shift in those early months at the *Press*. On my left was the glass separating the writer's front row from the broadcast booth, where the famous Bob Prince broadcast the games with Nellie King on KDKA radio.

I could see Prince's antics during every play and hear his raspy voice through the little transistor radio that Pirates PR guy Bill Guilfoyle always had at his seat to monitor the broadcast.

I'll never forget one night when Prince was going through his customary greetings to ill or hospitalized fans, as relayed to him by his staff.

Through the radio speaker, we heard, "I'd like to say hello to Joe and Mildred McGillicuddy in Dormont, who are wonderful Pirate fans and are both in the hospital, recovering from surgery."

With the last syllable barely out of his mouth, Prince put his finger on the cough button, stood up, leaned his skinny frame around the glass partition toward Smiz and me, and said, "You know, without those fuckin' shut-ins, you got fuckin' nothin.'"

On the road, Prince was known to secretly carry pre-mixed vodka screwdrivers in his carry-on bag, hidden in an old olives bottle, wrapped in a sock.

We were in the airport gate area early one morning, flying back to Pittsburgh after a late game the night before, when Prince pulled out the glass cylinder, twisted off the lid, happily poured his spiked breakfast drink into a cup, and then slid the bottle back into the sock.

I first witnessed this creative move when I was covering the Penguins for a month in place of our regular beat guy. Prince knew nothing about hockey, but after he and King had been fired contro-versially by KDKA, Pittsburgh's Channel 53 put "The Gunner" on the Penguins, well, because he was Bob Prince.

One night in the hotel bar, Johnny Wilson, the Penguin coach, convinced Prince that backchecking was checking someone in the back, which it wasn't, of course.

The next night on the Penguins' telecast, somebody slammed somebody else from behind and Prince said, "Well, now they're doing that backchecking thing again!"

I had called up Bob in his room one night to see if he had dinner plans. Happily, he didn't, and we ended up at Al's, a great steak house in East St. Louis. It was rather expensive, but since I had invited Bob, I reached for the check. Prince seized it first, however, and said, "Let me get that, laddie!"

I felt bad that he had picked up the tab since going to dinner was my idea, but the next day I spotted him in the hotel coffee shop, fin-ishing his lunch.

"Let me get that, Bob," I said.

He reluctantly allowed me to do so, and departed, telling me he'd see me on the team bus to the arena later.

I took the check to the cashier and gasped. A New York strip steak and three double vodka screwdrivers totaled up to $48—almost dou-ble my daily meal allowance.

It was worth every penny, though. As you can see, I'm still tell-ing the story.

———————

John Clayton was a youngster out of Duquesne, working at the *Press* covering mostly college stuff when I was there.

At one time John even did some tax returns of friends, including me, for extra cash. Ironically, at the end of our careers, he'd be the one with the impressive net worth and millions of YouTube viewers from his famous ESPN "Hey, Mom, I'm done with my segment" Metallica commercial.

As things turned out, with John being a few years younger and mostly covering either Pitt or Duquesne back then, sometimes he filled in for me on the Steelers beat, having even in those early days developed a staggering knowledge of personnel and league people.

Although the May 1978, day when Steelers coach Chuck Noll protested an NFL rule prohibiting shoulder pads at minicamp would put Clayton squarely on the national map—Chuck dared anyone to write it by parading his players in front of the media in pads—it had Steeler fans fuming when John did exactly that, eventually costing Pittsburgh a third-round draft pick as a penalty. The story became known as "Shouldergate."

Chuck had to know I would have reported the story, too, and when John called me after practice that day, I said he had no choice but to write what he saw. A couple of prominent Pittsburgh media people tried to talk John out of writing the story, but he held fast and took the eventual shrapnel from both Steeler fans and officials.

(Chuck would later contend that his displeasure with John came not from the lost draft choice, but that Clayton never talked to him for a response, and instead just reported the event to the NFL.)

John's sudden death in 2022 was very upsetting to many of us who knew him, especially because even at 67 he still seemed like that energetic young Pittsburgh kid who would give anything to cover his hometown heroes and devote more hours to his job than most guys were willing to spend.

There's never been a media person more knowledgeable about

the NFL, and player personnel in particular. John easily could have been an NFL general manager and a good one.

My first apartment in Pittsburgh was on noisy, dirty Ohio River Blvd, west of the city in Emsworth, a hard-core, truly hardhat suburb. It was a 1-bedroom place for $165 a month in 1974, with a carpet that smelled like a wet dog and too much traffic noise, but it was mine and I was on my own, working for a major newspaper in a big-league town. That a Perkins Steakhouse and the Wagon Wheel would become my major eating establishments was unfortunate but also temporary.

I upgraded nicely a year later to a small but classy apartment in a stately Victorian building in the trendy Shadyside neighborhood, which was Pittsburgh's version of Georgetown in those days, across from Sacred Heart Church. I could walk down Walnut Street and in five minutes visit the shops, restaurants, or bars. At the Encore, a jazz club, they offered a $5.95 dinner—NY Strip, baked potato, and salad. When I wasn't at the office or the ballgame, I was either there or at The Gazebo, a Jewish deli with a Reuben sandwich featuring thick rye bread saturated in butter and a wad of corned beef guaranteed to clog your arteries.

Whenever possible, I went to Three Rivers Stadium for Pirate games, seldom passing up a chance for free food and drinks in the media lounge and the opportunity to meet a few of my writing heroes coming through town, like Jim Murray or Red Smith, or broadcasters Vin Scully, Jack Buck, or Harry Caray.

When I first came to the *Press*, it was as an overnight desk man, working 11 p.m. to 7 a.m., unless occasionally you could manage being done earlier than that, and I got used to driving home up the Parkway East with the sun in my eyes. I worked that graveyard shift for about a year, volunteering for stories whenever I could just to get a byline, even if that meant working a double shift. But I was young, excited, and eager to do anything that pushed me closer to a writing position.

By the next year, while still not having totally broken free from the desk, at least now I was helping on the Steeler beat, doing home game sidebars with Musick, some Friday night high school football, and West Virginia home football games.

It tires me at this point just to recall it, but there were many weeks when I covered a Friday night high school football game west of Pittsburgh, drove to Morgantown, W. Va., immediately afterward, wrote the high school game story in my Quality Inn room there, then got up Saturday morning to cover the Mountaineers' 1 p.m. game. After that, it was back to Pittsburgh for the Sunday Steeler game.

That said, it sure beat the desk schedule before I was getting writing assignments—Friday 11 p.m. to 7 a.m., Saturday 4 p.m. to midnight, then Sunday overnight desk 11 p.m. to 7 a.m. It probably wasn't legal to overlap shifts like that, but there was no union for the writers, just the printers.

If it were possible to get sick from the awful coffee and what passed for food at the *Press* snack bar, surely that's when it would have happened. I somehow survived, although my stomach was never the same after that. I never knew coffee came in shades of gray.

Finally in the summer of 1976, when after what we all fondly called "The Great Steeler Write-off"—we all took a turn for a week writing training camp stories—I was selected to take over the Steelers beat, which opened up through Musick's move to the *Post-Gazette*. While taking over a team that had just won back-to-back Super Bowl titles at 25 years old was a little intimidating, the sheer excitement of my new job seemed to smooth out any nerves.

As I've said before, a lot of that I attribute to the Steelers being such a classy and friendly operation. Especially the Rooneys. I got along better with them than I did with my editors back at the office.

Beyond the football experiences of those years covering the Steelers, there was one other clear highlight.

Jessica.

Our first-born came at a most inconvenient time, professionally speaking, that is, as my then-wife Mary's due day was Tuesday of Super Bowl XIII week following the 1978 season, with the Steelers going for their third ring against the Cowboys in Miami on Jan 21, 1979.

Now you've got to understand that things were a bit different back then regarding Dads in the delivery room. Indeed, it was so rare that Myron Cope so warmly asked, "What the fuck are you going to do in there?"

Be there, Myron, and that's what I wanted to do.

Unfortunately, when I proceeded to spell it out for my executive sports editor at the *Press,* Don Dillman, he did not share the same sentiment.

"If you do go down there," he said, "you're not coming back."

Well, in that case, I said, I'm not going to go, and I didn't.

This is how John Clayton wound up covering Super Bowl XIII for me as the Steelers prevailed 35-31 over Dallas.

As for Mary and me, we ended up going to Magee Women's Hospital on Super Bowl Sunday night, shortly after the game concluded, having been timing contractions most of the second half. When we pulled into the parking lot at Magee, Steeler fans in hard hats with spinning red lights were celebrating down Fifth Avenue with cries of "DEE-fense, DEE-fense ... Here we go Steelers, HERE WE GO!"

Definitely surreal, we both agreed.

A couple of hours later, Jessica was born, and I was able to hold her only a moment or two after the delivery. I start to cry now just thinking about it, though Jessica is now in her 40s. I never regretted it for a second. There would be other Super Bowls, even ones with the team you cover participating. And there were.

In the Monday edition of the *Pittsburgh Press*, on page D-7, was a story, just below a feature on linebacker Dirt Winston, entitled: "It's a girl for Sheeleys."

When Jessica turned 30, I presented her with a framed copy of that famous front page, with one key alteration. We moved her birth story to the front page and re-shot the photo. It hangs today in Jessica's office and it's my favorite front page of all time. Here I go, crying again.

It's a Dad thing. I know you guys understand.

CHAPTER 5

THE ROONEYS

I
T WAS A GREAT RIDE, COVERING THE PITTSBURGH STEELERS
and the Rooney family during the 1970s.

The Chief, Art Rooney, Sr., even attended my first wedding.
When he died at age 87 in 1988, I had moved to Atlanta by then and
was covering the Falcons. The team's owner, Rankin Smith, Sr., offered to take me along on his private jet to attend Mr. Rooney's wake
in Pittsburgh, and I happily accepted.

We left a regional Atlanta airport at about 11 a.m. and were
home before 4 pm. Now that's the way to fly!

I'll never forget walking up the steps of the church with Rankin
and stopping to chat with the late Commissioner Pete Rozelle, who
was puffing on a cigarette before the service.

"Let me get this straight," Pete said. "Rankin gave YOU a ride
on his plane? Boy, Mr. Rooney really did bring people together,
didn't he?"

As he did with many personal acquaintances, The Chief sent
me signed postcards for several years after I left Pittsburgh and,

of course, I still have all of them. I'm sure my grandkids will enjoy looking at them when I'm gone.

Even in his mid-70s, The Chief would brave the cold weather at Three Rivers Stadium and stand outside for hours at practice, where cold concrete underneath the AstroTurf penetrated everyone's shoes. And, if you happened to seek warmer refuge before the end of practice and The Chief happened to see you ducking into the tunnel, he would chuckle and ask playfully behind those twinkling eyes, "Too cold for youse out there?"

One early winter day at practice, running back Mike Collier was turning the corner on a sweep and accidentally took out The Chief on the sidelines. Brushing himself off, the former boxer and saloon fighter stood back up, helped by several stunned coaches and players, and calmly resumed watching his team.

A couple of days later, Collier was cut. We were never sure whether it was because he ran over The Chief or because the collision wasn't impactful enough to hurt an old man.

Dan Rooney, The Chief's oldest son, was vice president and GM when I started covering the Steelers and was always the picture of class. More than any other sports executive I had ever encountered, Dan understood why writers wrote what they did, and he didn't take it personally. He knew we were working to please our bosses, just like everyone else in Pittsburgh. He was also a big fan of the sports pages, and he would read the "negative" stories as religiously as the ones that praised his team. He liked asking your opinion on some non-Steeler story he had been reading. He was a sports fan.

I would still occasionally call Dan many years after I left Pittsburgh and did so following the Steelers' last Super Bowl victory in 2009. He greeted me on the phone as though we had just spoken the day before. That was Dan Rooney.

The fact that the Rooneys were just regular guys made them unique in sports ownership and they made me comfortable from the start.

Hey, you've got to love true Pittsburgh guys who wear long underwear under their dress shirts in the winter and have been known to dot them with tobacco juice stains.

I didn't know Art, Jr (Artie) as well as I did Dan, largely because he wasn't front and center except at draft time, but he was a great guy, too. Art II, the owner now, was just starting in the organization when I was the beat guy, but I always figured he would be the main man at some point.

Dick Haley, who served as the Steelers' draft boss during their glory years, was also fun to cover. I remember 1976 when that crazy guy crashed his little plane into the stands in Baltimore just minutes after the Steelers' playoff game concluded against the Colts. Had the plane slammed into those upper deck seats just a bit earlier, when the game was still going on, hundreds of fans could have been in danger.

Said Haley dryly, "We would have had to have Ernie (Holmes) shoot it down."

Joe Gordon, the long-time Steeler publicist, was the Steeler official I spent the most time with and was widely recognized as one of the top PR guys in the NFL. Joe was a tough but extremely fair PR guy, and I highly valued his friendship, the same as I did later when I moved to Atlanta and the Falcons' Charlie Dayton became my daily connection with the team. Today they're both deservedly in the Pro Football Hall of Fame.

Joe's job had an unusual twist to it, given the Steelers' unique situation with their media people, the smaller circulation reporters, in particular. According to The Chief's wishes, all beat writers were allowed on the team charters, regardless of their paper's stature. The way Mr. Rooney figured it, those little papers were loyal to the Steelers when they were lousy, and now that the Steelers were the NFL's biggest story, he wasn't going to abandon them and their readers.

So, as a result, the Steelers took them on the team plane every road game, didn't charge them airfare, and even paid their hotel bill, minus extras. Truth is, those papers from McKeesport or Irwin or Greensburg could not have afforded to attend road games without this arrangement and the Rooneys wanted them to be there to experience the good times, after the dreadful "Same Old Steelers" years of the past.

The Pittsburgh papers were in a different situation, with reasonable budgets and, well, the need to exhibit more objectivity. As a result, when the *Press* or *Post-Gazette* guy rode, we asked to be billed regular airfare from the Steelers. I'm not sure they always did it, but we were supposed to request it. (To be perfectly honest, as cool as it was for a kid in his mid-20s to be traveling with these future Hall of Famers, I was never comfortable in that team plane environment. I always said I wanted to be able to leave the room if necessary. This was the team's domain, not mine, and I often felt like I was eavesdropping.)

That's not to say that life on the Steeler charter was a negative experience. We enjoyed incredible access to the players and got to know them considerably better because of such proximity. It was fairly common for talkative guys like Terry Bradshaw or Mike Wagner to stop by your seat to chat. I used to play gin with running back Jack Deloplaine on occasion. Under our rules, the game did not end until the wheels touched the ground, which made for some crazy final moments as cards were being knocked off tray tables and onto the floor.

As I said, things were a lot different then. It was even customary in the '70s and '80s for the team to take the Steeler reporters out to dinner the night before the game and, of course, pick up the entire tab. Even the Pittsburgh writers stood back and allowed this gesture. While this might sound hypocritical, can you imagine how insulted Joe Gordon would have been if Vito Stellino, my *Post-Gazette* competition, or I had asked when the bill came, "What do we owe you?"

We let it slide and we never felt compromised. We could still write our tough stories, and we did. Joe Gordon and I had our share of vigorous discussions, but never anything unkind or very uncomfortable.

Even back then, with a dozen or so people eating at one of the road city's best restaurants, it was a pricey undertaking. At an Italian place named Mario's in Dallas, one night before a Cowboys game, Dave Ailes of Greensburg and I saw the bill, which exceeded $1,000, pass by us on the way to Gordon's seat at the head of the table. In to-day's dollars, that's probably a $5,000 tab.

"Well," Ailes decided, "we just ate a used car."

It's only after you cover other pro sports teams that you truly realize how special the Rooneys were then and still are today. I was very lucky to have landed that desk job in 1974 with the *Press* and even more fortunate that it opened a path to covering the finest team in NFL history and the finest owners ever, in any sport.

In 1975, when I was Phil Musick's backup on the Steeler beat and still semi-tied to the desk, I occasionally did his off-day story, spending time at both St. Vincent College during training camp and at the Steeler offices during the regular season. By the time I took over the beat in 1976 when Musick left for the *Post-Gazette*, I had met both The Chief and Dan a few times and covered several games at Three Rivers with Phil.

"You can stop introducing yourself to The Chief," said gravel-voiced Ed Kiely, the publicist emeritus. "He knows who you are now."

Which felt pretty good, I had to admit.

CHAPTER 6

TERRY BRADSHAW

I F I WERE EVER TRYING TO REACH TERRY BRADSHAW FOR A STORY and had left a phone message, when he called me back, which he always did, sometimes it would start with him identifying himself by asking playfully, "Hoss, who's your favorite football player of all time?"

Terry was always great with me when I covered the Steelers as a young kid in my mid-20s. He'd stop by in the press room at St. Vincent College after post-dinner team meetings and routinely spend an hour or so just chatting or providing inside info, usually off the record, to a rookie beat man still trying to find his way around the NFL's dominant team.

He told me things I might use in the next day's paper, as long as he was OK with it. He told me things I've never told anyone to this day. We hit it off immediately and it was a lot of fun.

Usually, that is.

I made the mistake of tossing around the football with him for a few minutes at practice one day and almost got my nose broken in the process. The ball made a hissing sound as it approached too close to my face, and this was probably a half-speed pass. His hands were so strong that he could easily place his forefinger on the point of the football for extra velocity, rocketing it downfield as powerfully as anyone in the league.

I took the next ball from him well to the side, away from my body, and even then the laces nearly split open the palm of my hand. Needing no more proof of the danger, I flipped the football to a ballboy and went back to watching practice and scribbling in my notebook.

After Terry broke a bone in his left wrist in a game at Houston in 1977, my then-wife, Mary, was waiting at the Pittsburgh airport that night with Bradshaw's second wife, JoJo Starbuck, the ice skater, when the Steelers' plane returned. My ex-wife knew something about medicine, being a nurse anesthetist, and it was clear that JoJo did not when she said to Mary, "At first, they said it was only fractured, but now I hear it's broken!"

Sometimes when I rode the Steelers' charter, I had to work on the plane at my seat on the longer flights, then retype my stories when I got to the office hours later. These were manual typewriter days, before laptops, and clattering keys made a good bit of racket.

Sometimes Terry would appear at the seatback just ahead of me and ask me how my story was coming.

"Not great," I might say, smiling. "I'm trying to make you look good and it's been a struggle so far."

After a few minutes, Terry would go back to his seat, with a familiar trail remaining to remind me of his chuckling, razzing visit. Little dots of tobacco juice were often sprinkled across the page.

When Bradshaw was inducted into the Hall of Fame in 1989, on Saturday morning, Aug. 5, I was at the Hall of Fame game in Canton, Ohio, between the Redskins and the Bills later that Saturday afternoon to both chronicle my old pal's honor and do a story on running back Gerald Riggs, who had gone to the Redskins from Atlanta. We partied with Terry very late the night before and might have managed an hour's sleep, being seriously hung over. But it was a blast, and as Jimmy Cagney once said, "You can sleep when you're dead."

I had been working for a few days on a long Bradshaw centerpiece story for the Sunday *Atlanta Journal-Constitution* and it was almost done. I was doing some final editing on the story while watching the game in that stifling hot press box when suddenly I noticed a pool of brown liquid oozing out from under my Radio Shack laptop.

As it turns out, somebody had spilled a Coke and the mess was spreading quickly, basically wiping out my computer and, of course, the story. No backups were available then. No printout. Nothing. I was totally screwed. The story was gone, as was my computer.

At right about that point, Bradshaw appeared from behind me, slapped me on the back, and shouted, "How's the story going, hoss?"

I was barely able to speak, my face flushed from the disaster, and I excused myself to figure out whether I could somehow pull off a miracle, with no sleep, my head pounding, and a Sunday deadline approaching.

When it should have been a fun time all around, it was probably the worst day of my professional life.

Although I was able to borrow my buddy John Czarnecki's laptop, which he didn't need until later when filing for the *Dallas Morning News,* I had to reconstruct the story from memory. All I had was my notebook.

I retreated to an old photo darkroom at the top of the stadium, gathered my thoughts as best I could, and started writing again.

As it turned out, I only missed the early deadline and, considering everything, managed to assemble a decent recovery story from my notebook notes. Sending the story was also a problem because John's computer configurations were not the same, but finally, everything got to my office by about 8:30.

By the time I arrived at the reception where I was to meet Bradshaw, the food was gone, so a few beers and some chips became my friends. I would have paid handsomely for a couple of Advil.

I tried to explain the exhausting ordeal to Terry, but I'm not sure if it sank in. He was still flying from the day's event, and good for him. He certainly earned it, even if my computer choked in the big moment.

There were times after Terry first retired that I truly felt bad for him. When the analyst-in-the-booth role didn't work out with CBS, the network had him off doing mid-week features at NFL camps. He made a stop at the Falcons' team facility for a story, and I could tell he was uncomfortable and unsettled about what the future might hold.

But then it all changed. He became part of the NFL Today team for the CBS Sunday pre-game show, eventually went to FOX for huge money, and remains there.

In his 70s now, he has done it all—movies, commercials, TV, talk shows, everything, even a Vegas act—and I couldn't be happier for him.

For me, he will always be that guy at Steeler training camp in 1976, as big as there was in the NFL, just trying to help out a rookie on the beat.

And yes, hoss, you were my favorite.

CHAPTER 7

MYRON COPE

I F YOU AREN'T FROM PITTSBURGH OR AREN'T FAMILIAR WITH Myron Cope, I feel sorry for you, because he WAS Pittsburgh and you missed quite an opportunity.

While becoming a part of Steeler legend as the team's color man on radio broadcasts for 35 years, Myron Cope understandably became the subject of some hilarious stories—some I can even tell you after all these years.

I know this. I attended far too many last calls with Myron on the night before Steeler games. I stayed out much too late. Luckily, I was usually just drinking beer instead of trying to keep up with Myron's double vodka martinis. Otherwise, I probably wouldn't be alive to type this.

But ever since Myron passed in 2008, I've recounted many of our adventures with great fondness, and I laugh just as hard now at them as I did then.

Myron had a mangled left ear and didn't hear very well from that side, so when you were at dinner with him, he always ordered you to "sit near my good ear" if he was interested in what you were saying.

Well, I guess his bad ear was closest to the front of the room at the 1978 PGA Championship at Oakmont Country Club when PGA Tour Communications head John Morris addressed the assembled working media.

"For those of you who are interested," Morris said softly, "I'm sorry to announce that Pope Paul has died."

The writers stopped hammering their typewriters, bowed their heads momentarily, and then went back to their stories.

At the back of the room, Cope looked astonished and said to his buddy, Vic Ketchman, of the *Irwin Standard-Observer*, "He was just a young man......He couldn't have been more than 38. I just saw him do a beer commercial."

Whereupon Ketchman said, "WHAAAAATTT?"

Replied Cope, "He just said that Boog Powell died!"

Huge laughter ensued, which you don't often hear after a death announcement.

The kicker to this story always was, why the hell would anybody care to announce that Boog Powell had died, even if he just did?

A preseason trip in 1976 brought the Steelers to Washington, D.C., which meant an expensive Friday night dinner (for the Steelers, because they always treated) at an old standby, the famous Duke Zeibert's. More drinks always came afterward, but at least with a Saturday night game, you had all day to recover.

With the post-dinner bar crowd departing, it dwindled to just me and Cope—a dangerous pairing, to be sure. Heading out on foot, we ended up at a local watering hole called "The Déjà vu Bar."

Sipping his martini, Cope looked around the room with semi-glazed-over eyes and declared, "The Déjà vu? Heh, I think I've been here before."

A couple of drinks later, we called a cab to take us back to the Marriott, the team hotel. He dropped us off and I bid adieu to Cope for the night.

Then the fun started. I got to my floor and could not find my room, where I had visited briefly to check in that afternoon and had received a key bearing the room number.

Heading back to the lobby, I searched for possibly a different elevator tower than I had taken before, figuring that might be the problem. Nope. My room still was not there.

So, I went back to the front desk and explained the problem, whereupon the clerk said, "Which Marriott are you supposed to be in?"

"Uh, the Key Bridge Marriott?"

"Well," he said, "this is the Twin Bridges Marriott."

Oops.

I called a cab and was dropped off at the correct Marriott, telling the cab driver as I left, "Hey, if you want another fare, I recommend going back to the Twin Bridges Marriott and looking for a guy who sounds like he's got a clothespin stuck in his throat."

I don't know if he ever did, but the next day, fighting a serious hangover and thankful for an evening game, I was headed down to the pool, seeking some Vitamin D sunshine. Suddenly, the elevator stopped at a floor on the way down, revealing none other than a stunned Cope in his exact clothes from the night before.

Laughing, I said, "Hey, Myron, what are they getting for rooms at the Twin Bridges Marriott these days?"

As the doors closed, Myron said something about me being full of shit, but I have never doubted that he slept at the wrong Marriott that night, in no condition to regroup to find the correct one.

Amazingly, he told the story on the air shortly thereafter, minus a few details, of course.

For a Steelers game at Cleveland that same year, for some reason a few of us decided to fly instead of taking the easy two-hour drive. Cope was among those of us at the airport after the game and a slightly delayed flight meant only one thing—more time in the bar.

I had asked Myron earlier if he could give me a ride from the Pittsburgh airport back to my apartment, which was just across the street from WTAE, his TV station, on Ardmore Boulevard, and he happily obliged.

Well, when the second or third martini had reached his lips in the Cleveland Airport bar, I was questioning the intelligence of my request. After we landed in Pittsburgh and Cope required six tries to leave his airport parking space, I knew I was in serious trouble.

Halfway up the parkway toward downtown, Cope was swerving all over the road, barely missing the guardrail, and I hastily decided on Plan B. Drop me off downtown at the newspaper office instead of continuing this drunken madness, I said, and I'll take a cab from there.

Which he did, then basically passed out in his car at the curb.

Somehow Myron managed to do a newscast at 11, though I never saw him until the next day at Chuck Noll's Monday press luncheon.

He came up to me afterward, pointed to his chin, and said, "Go ahead, hit me. Give me one right here."

"For what?" I said.

"For leaving you at the airport."

Petrified that he was more unconscious than I ever imagined, I said, "Myron, I had you drop me off downtown because I thought you might get me killed! Don't you remember?"

"Oh, yeah, that's right. I remember."

He didn't, of course, and I thanked God one more time for keeping me safe.

Most of Cope's antics were hilarious and harmless. Like his commercials for Stop-and-Go convenience stores, riding in a little shopping cart pushed by Steeler lineman Jon Kolb. Or swimming the filthy Monongahela River to satisfy a bet. Myron even gave me credit in his book for tagging the Cincinnati Bengals as the "Bungles" during their lowly days.

He wasn't happy with some of the things I wrote, mainly because they differed greatly with how far he would have crept toward objectivity as someone who admittedly rooted for the Steelers. But we always remained friends.

When the Steelers lost a third-round draft pick in 1978 for Coach Chuck Noll's decision to challenge the NFL's rules on wearing shoulder pads at mini-camp, the coach claimed there were those in the Steeler media (namely myself and John Clayton, who wrote the story on my off day) "working for the other people."

What Chuck meant was, the Oakland Raiders and Al Davis, which was, of course, totally ridiculous.

Not surprisingly, Cope thought the lead of my Sunday story, which ran under a giant headline that proclaimed, "Noll Charges Espionage in Shoulder Pads Affair," was out of bounds when I led with, "Richard Nixon is alive and well and coaching the Steelers."

Heck, and it probably was. But so was Chuck's claim.

With a chance to do it over, we both probably would have taken a deep breath and done something less reactionary.

After the most famous play in Steeler history, Franco Harris' "Immaculate Reception" in the 1972 playoff miracle against Oakland, Myron was stationed at a Three Rivers pay phone and waiting excitedly to do his post-game show on WTAE radio at about 5 p.m.

Waiting for his cue from the radio station, by 4:55 he had heard nothing on the other end. Still on hold with silence at two minutes before 5. Finally, at just before 5, a voice on the other end was saying, "And now, live, from Three Rivers Stadium, here's Myron Cope!"

Trouble was, Cope heard nothing on his end and now asked frantically, his words going out over the air, "Hello…Hello…WHAT THE FUCK?"

The voice, of course, was unmistakably Myron's, and when people heard it releasing an F-bomb so clearly and suddenly on their way home, some cars reportedly ran off the road into ditches.

When Myron showed up at the Press Club that night, his station owner was dead serious when he told him, "We could go to jail for this."

"Who goes?" Myron said. "Me or you?"

"Me!" the station owner said.

"Good," Cope said. "I'll send you a fruitcake."

There were at least a couple of things that a lot of people didn't know about Myron. Number one, he was an incredibly gifted writer for the *Pittsburgh Post-Gazette* and then several national magazines before his unexpected turn to a broadcasting career. His profiles on Muhammad Ali and Howard Cosell, for example, were fantastic. You should read his book, "Double Yoi!" to learn more about this talented, unique little man who at times was even bigger than the Steelers.

People who loved Myron also might not know about his soft, charitable side. His son, Danny, who was autistic, attended the Allegheny Valley School, which Myron designated as the recipient of profits from sales of his Terrible Towel.

It has raised more than $6 million for the school.

CHAPTER 8

JOE GREENE

I N THE LOBBY OF HIS SAINT VINCENT COLLEGE DORMITORY ROOM shortly after lunch in August of 1978 during Steeler training camp, I waited for Joe Greene to come downstairs. While I knew I had a great story on my hands—and I was pretty sure that nobody else in the media knew about it—I was dreading a confrontation with the imposing defensive tackle in this unsettling hunt for a necessary comment.

When he finally came off the elevator and headed for the door, I approached him cautiously, being the young Steelers beat guy I was. At 6-1, maybe 180 then, I was no shrimp, yet a true pencil-neck compared to these gentlemen who scarfed down multiple NY strip steaks at dinner as though mere sliders.

I started the conversation slowly, acknowledging my realization that he was still struggling at training camp with his left arm and shoulder, which then wouldn't allow him to curl even 25 pounds, let alone grab an offensive tackle by one arm and toss aside a quarterback with the other. Beyond that, however, I knew he had just gone for a neurological exam at Presbyterian Hospital in Pittsburgh that same day.

Now while I eventually would develop a fine relationship with Joe and, like all of the beat writers, considered him an interview go-to-guy (there was nobody on the team more expressive and thoughtful), on this day I was directly questioning his very existence and performance.

"WHO YOU BEEN TALKIN' TO?" Mean Joe Greene asked me.

While I was tempted to just say, "Oh, never mind," and slip out the side door, I persisted. There was no turning back from the story. Plus, I had plenty of info to write it without Joe's quotes. I just wanted his thoughts in the story.

While trusting sources can be risky business, this time there were no such worries. Although my first wife, Mary, eventually would want a divorce, she still liked me back then and just wanted to help her husband with his work. A nurse at Presbyterian, she had seen Joe walk in for the exam and called me almost immediately.

(I am finally admitting this only because the late Myron Cope always suspected that's how I got the story, but I always told him, "Oh, right, Myron. Like I need my wife to get stories for me. Get serious. Give me a little more credit than that.")

Realizing I had my information correct, Joe didn't try to say I was wrong, but he didn't say anything else for the record, either, and walked out.

Mission accomplished, I guess. I still had all my teeth.

And the story, which I was working on when the phone rang in my dorm room.

It was Dan Rooney, then the Steelers' vice president, who asked if I could meet him somewhere to chat.

I knew it was probably regarding the Joe Greene story, and we suggested a campus building away from the players' dorms.

When we got there, Dan said he felt it important to give me some background on the Joe Greene issue so I would understand the delicacy of the matter.

One faction on the team, he said, respected Joe so much, it didn't matter whether he was 100 percent or 10 percent effective. The other side said, screw it if he can't play, there are younger guys who can.

Well, as it turns out, the pro-Joe Greene side prevailed and Greene remained, finally regaining his strength late in the season. But the story apparently made me the bad guy.

In 1978 the Steelers' home opener was against Seattle and my new in-laws, John and Marge Kelley, were among those in the Three Rivers Stadium crowd.

As the game was about to begin, the usual excited murmur drifted through the crowd, but something a little different was being heard up in the press box. I noticed that a buzz was traveling toward me from my left, and as I glanced up I noticed my fellow writers taking turns pointing to the left corner of the end zone, where a sign spelled out ever so clearly in bold, capital letters:

GLENN SHEELEY SUCKS!

I never did ask John and Marge what they thought of this summation regarding their new son-in-law, but it probably wasn't going to help me at Thanksgiving dinner.

It was weird to see something so derogatory, especially considering, well, the incredible quality of the sign. I mean, this wasn't something the guy scribbled at the last minute from the back of his truck. This was well done, perfectly lettered, big, and bold, and obviously was completed beforehand and transported to Three Rivers for the big unveiling.

As I soon realized, it was a result of the Joe Greene story and this particular fan's assumption that I was anti-Mean Joe, which couldn't have been further from the truth.

In any case, as I noticed at halftime, suddenly the sign was gone, and I saw Dan Rooney a few moments later.

"Let me ask you something, Dan," I said. "If the sign had said 'Glenn Sheeley Stinks,' would you have taken it down?"

After all, in the mid-1970s, the use of the word "sucks" was considered a lot more profane than is the case nowadays.

Dan grinned and said, "I think you know the answer to that question, Glenn."

He was mean, of course, only on the field. Otherwise, Joe Greene was a gentle guy in voice and mannerisms. On the field, he could grab an offensive lineman's balls with one hand and pull down a running back with the other. In the locker room or away from Three Rivers Stadium, he spoke in soft, descriptive sentences and was a master at summing up emotions in a modicum of words, getting to the point more quickly than he arrived at a quarterback's collapsing pocket.

I was talking to Joe at his locker one day in the corner of the Steelers' locker room. I had just pulled up a stool next to his No. 75 cubicle when safety Glen Edwards, having seen me, came over to our side of the room, stark naked, and began screaming at me about my story of the previous day. I had quoted defensive coordinator Bud Carson as saying Edwards "had lost a step." Harsh criticism from his coach, to be sure, but Carson never was one to pull his punches. Like most players, Edwards decided to beat up on the messenger instead of going to the coach.

"You motherfucker, I ought to kill you!" Edwards said. "Write that shit about me in the paper, motherfucker, I ought to kill you!"

After a minute or two of this bizarre tirade, Edwards, screaming so everyone could hear and dangling his dick in front of us, eventually returned to his locker, still muttering.

Silent during the outburst, Joe then turned to me and said, "Where were we?"

Joe was so good with interviews; I was always stunned that he never succeeded as a TV analyst. He was in my top three all-time for best quotes, most expressively offered, and availability even after tough losses.

I always thought he would have been a great head coach, but in retrospect, I'm kind of glad it never happened. Had he not won enough games, it would have tainted the solid, sensational image of Joe Greene, especially in Pittsburgh, and that truly would have been a shame.

CHAPTER 9

JACK LAMBERT

ALTHOUGH IT MIGHT NOT SEEM POSSIBLE GIVEN TODAY'S locked-down, sequestered security of Super Bowl Week, it wasn't always like this. Time was when the Super Bowl teams were on their own for at least a couple of days upon arrival at the Super Bowl site, rather than being locked in their hotel rooms with NFL security people on each floor.

This was very much the case in January of 1980, when the Pittsburgh Steelers arrived in Newport Beach, Calif., to begin preparations for Super Bowl XIV. It was so loose then that the players, though they had a curfew, could do whatever they so desired Monday night. The NFL police didn't clamp down on them until Photo Day, as it was called then, on Tuesday.

As a result, I was at the bar at the Newport Beach Marriott with Jack Lambert, the infamous Steeler middle linebacker, who was chain-smoking cigarettes and throwing down beers at an impressive pace, especially considering what was at stake. But, then again, this was a guy who usually chugged beers in the sauna after a game, ignoring any regard toward fending off dehydration.

So, here we are trading beers and cigarettes six days before the Super Bowl and this Southern California girl who figures Lambert is somebody important, squeezes between some Steeler fans near the bar and actually asks him, "What's your sign?"

Without hesitation, Lambert sucks on the cigarette, gulps a beer, and says to her, "Feces."

I fell off my barstool, howling, and Lambert says, "You liked that, huh?"

Yeah, I did, but there was more.

The girl follows up with, "Really? I'm a Libra!"

Jack Lambert was the most intense, most competitive athlete I ever knew or saw, and I think a lot of people who covered the NFL back then would agree. Although as people who regularly covered the Steelers, we observed more examples of Lambert's insatiable, angry desire than the national media, it was fairly obvious.

In 1976 the Steelers had a season-opening game against the Raiders in Oakland, and they lost 31-28 when quarterback Ken Stabler brought them back for the upset.

An hour later, as we were waiting for the last bus to leave for the airport and the flight back to Pittsburgh, Lambert was at the back of the vehicle, sitting across the rear seats with his dad, who often made road trips and was allowed to ride on the charter. Jack, of course, did not have his front teeth in place, which always made him look more monstrous.

"Gimme a six-pack," Lambert said, "and I'd play those motherfuckers again right now."

And he would have.

Three seasons later, the Steelers were leaving California in a much better mood, having just won Super Bowl XIV over the Los Angeles Rams. Exiting the Newport Beach Marriott the Monday after, Jack was holding my 11-month-old daughter, Jessica, just before he boarded the team bus.

Jessica, who was born on the night the Steelers defeated Dallas in Super Bowl XIII, had no clue she was the envy of every kid in Pittsburgh.

Too bad there were no smartphones then. It would have been a great photo to show her even now.

CHAPTER 10

CHUCK NOLL

I HADN'T SEEN CHUCK NOLL IN MANY YEARS WHEN SUDDENLY I noticed a familiar face on the putting green at the Atlanta Athletic Club in the mid-'90s. Unbeknownst to me, the famous Steeler coach was in town for a celebrity golf tournament. Even more surprisingly, Noll greeted me more like a legitimate old friend, not someone who parried with him almost daily back in the '70s. He offered me a warm laugh and extended his hand.

"How the hell are you?" he asked with a wide grin.

Seeing his face so brightened, I remember thinking how unfortunate that it took me leaving Pittsburgh, him retiring, and golf, of all things, to bring out the personality in this stoic man who coached the best team in NFL history.

I believe he was living in Hilton Head then and was really into sailing with his wife, Marianne. I had even heard they were going to sail up the East Coast from South Carolina and my first thought upon hearing that was, hmm, is there any weather that might make this notoriously stubborn man turn around?

"Whatever it takes," Noll always liked to say of his coaching mission.

This isn't to say there were never light moments with Chuck Noll when I was covering the Steelers back then. When we would congregate for lunch in the small kitchen of the Steeler offices at Three Rivers Stadium, he loved pulling out a factoid for everyone's entertainment. While it was probably merely to let these people who criticized his every move know that he just might be smarter than them, it was, nonetheless, often still amusing.

One day, completely out of nowhere, he said to a few of us, "Did you ever notice how you have to adjust the mirror of your car in the morning, always tilting it up a bit?"

OK, Chuck, maybe, but where are you going with this?

"That's because you're sitting up straighter than you were when you last drove," he said. "People tend to naturally slump a bit at the end of the day."

We used to call those Nollisms. Occasionally, he would even follow them with a distinct belly laugh. I kid you not. It was very distinctive, and I can still hear it in my head.

Contrast that with 1976, when Noll made his infamous "criminal element" remarks at a Monday press conference following hits by the Raiders' George Atkinson on Steelers receiver Lynn Swann in the season opener a day earlier, prompting a lawsuit by Raiders owner Al Davis.

Or when Noll flipped out in 1978 after illegally putting the team in shoulder pads before a mini-camp workout as a protest to the NFL policy, eventually losing a third-round draft choice for the move. (It was a stupid rule, most everyone agreed, but only Noll had the balls to challenge it.)

The late John Clayton of ESPN fame was occasionally my off-day guy on the Steelers beat back then. He saw it at practice and reported it in the next day's paper. When I followed up the following day, I was interviewing Noll in his office when he suggested there were those of us "working for the other people" and angrily walked out of his own office with my tape recorder still running.

He was a complicated man with a love of wine, sailing, scuba diving, photography, classical music, and literature. He was quick to laugh at things that amused him; it just didn't happen often enough. Maybe that was the influence of studying under Paul Brown, another very serious man.

There were times when Chuck did make me laugh, though. Back in 1976, when the Steelers played in what would be the last College All-Star Game, which ended in a mind-boggling downpour and lightning storm at Chicago's Soldier Field, a soaked Noll was addressing reporters in a frenzied locker room. When a very pushy Chicago radio person stuck a tape recorder just inches from Noll's face, the irritated coach punched the OFF button on it and said, "I MIGHT talk to you later."

Other things should have drawn a laugh from Chuck, but for some reason did not. He remained stone-faced at a pre-Super Bowl press conference one year, when famously flakey LA Rams Fred Dryer and Jack Youngblood, dressed up like old-time reporters, asked from the back of the room, "Chuck, is the zone defense here to stay and, if not, where is it going?"

It always saddened me that Noll and Terry Bradshaw had such a turbulent relationship. They should have been mutually admiring each other, given their lofty places in NFL history, but instead they butted heads. Together, however, they won four Super Bowls, so something must have worked.

You might not know that Chuck suffered from Alzheimer's for

several years before he died in 2014. I hated to learn this, having been witness to the man's intelligence and football genius for so many years.

Do I wish he would have shown a warmer side? Sure, but I guess that's how he felt he had to coach and lead. I was too young then to grasp that—just 25 when I took over the Steelers beat in 1976, hugely energetic and journalistically bolstered in the post-Watergate era.

At least, as we were both standing on a golf course, I eventually got to see that twinkle in Chuck Noll's eyes. Better late than never, I guess.

CHAPTER 11

JOHN MADDEN

I's been suggested that maybe things should have been reversed. Maybe husky John Madden, who had the ruddy look of an Irish bartender, should have been the Steelers' head coach, while secretive and stoic Chuck Noll in the 1970s seemed more programmed for work on that island known as the Raiders organization.

I only really got to know John Madden after he retired from coaching the Raiders and became TV's most popular NFL analyst ever. I covered him for a few years as the Steeler beat man with the *Pittsburgh Press* but didn't spend any time with him outside of press conferences and post-game interviews until he became the Miller Lite pitchman and rewrote the book on providing NFL color on TV.

And, unlike my relationship with his boss, the Raiders' bizarre Al Davis, which was always a bit combative due to the Steeler-Raider rivalry and its assorted controversies, Madden and I always had a lot of laughs together, be it in person or by phone.

He even recommended me to his publisher to co-write a book with him in the early '80s, when I was in Atlanta. It was supposed to be called "John Madden's 100 Favorite Players" and while it would not likely have been a writing masterpiece, I was excited to be part-nering with Madden. Unfortunately, though, shortly after we started doing our background work, the project fell apart at the publisher's end for some unexplained reason.

We had spoken several times, though, during that period when John was taking the "Madden Bus" all around the country as an al-ternative to flying. One night we were discussing something about the book, just as he said he was driving through Midland, Tex., and in the middle of a sentence, he said, "Shit, my fuckin' satellite dish just blew off!"

Madden's desire to avoid airplanes was not merely as a nervous flyer concerned about safety. It was claustrophobia, which bothered him when he flew on the Raiders' trips, but he gutted his way through it with cocktails and anything else he needed. When the choice be-came his as a broadcaster, he took to the road.

Not only did traveling this way appeal to Madden, who loved to people-watch in hotel lobbies until he got too popular to pull it off, but it also kept the networks from forcing him to, say, do games in LA and New York on consecutive nights. Be it by bus or by train, Madden's trips took a couple of days, and he liked the slow pace, watching games or movies on TV until, well, his dish blew off into the desert.

I only realized the scope of John's claustrophobia during a car trip we took from LA to his home in Danville, Calif., in 1986. For most of the trip, it was just Madden and me in his Mercedes, zooming up Interstate 5 through tumbleweeds and roadside cafes. A buddy of his rode part of the trip, snoozing in the back seat, but mostly it was just us. I think I filled five micro-cassette tapes talking to John. It was awesome.

We stopped for gas at a convenience store, and I pumped while he went in for soft drinks in white Levi's and untied running shoes.

This being at the height of his Miller Lite/NFL popularity, patrons were gawking in disbelief as Madden prowled the aisles of the store, grabbing bags of chips and cans of Bubble-Up.

When we stopped for lunch at the Harris Ranch in Coalinga, Calif., about halfway to the Bay Area, we were sitting at a table, which was open at one side, where Madden pulled up a chair.

"I couldn't sit where you're sitting," he said, meaning toward the wall. "No way."

Now, that is serious claustrophobia.

It's a wonder he lasted all those years flying on the Raiders' charters. Panic attacks were common.

The day before our 5-hour drive to Northern California, Madden had played in the Raiders' charity golf tournament at Riviera Country Club in Pacific Palisades, Calif., near LA, as a favor to Coach Tom Flores. Speaking afterward, Madden was clearly more comfortable with a microphone in his hands than a golf club. "Why the hell," he asked, "would anybody want to play this game?"

We chatted in the clubhouse with Raider superfan James Garner, the actor, who said he loved being a member at Riviera, but "you can't get a fuckin' tee time." Hmm, stuff you never heard on *The Rockford Files*, to be sure.

When Madden picked me up the next morning at my hotel, the LAX Airport Hyatt, he shouted from the passenger side window as I approached the car, "Did you feel it?"

"Feel what?" I said.

"The earthquake!" Madden said excitedly. "The hangers were banging back and forth in my closet!"

"Never felt a thing," I said. "I had a few beers and went to bed."

It didn't really surprise me that Madden had been a light sleeper. Considering his constant cigarette buzz and generally jazzed-up metabolism, I was surprised he slept at all.

The trip culminated in Danville, Calif., and Madden's home in swank Blackhawk Country Club, where at the time Billy Martin and Rollie Fingers were among his neighbors. John and his wife had His and Hers golf carts in the garage. Life was good. And no Al Davis to question his every move.

I'll never forget the Monday Super Bowl press conference after the Raiders beat the Vikings in 1977. Madden was speaking before a large cluster of microphones that had been taped together at the hotel ballroom podium. A couple of times one of the microphones broke loose from the group and Madden had to stop talking to secure it again.

"Every time I lie," Madden laughed, "this thing falls down."

A moment later, a reporter asked Madden to comment on the popular opinion that Davis actually pulls the strings with team decisions, not the head coach.

Right as Madden began his adamant denial, suddenly the microphone fell again.

Everyone roared with laughter, Madden included.

Our executives at the *AJC* in 1986 were eager to capitalize on the Madden Miller Lite mania and wanted Madden for the cover of our Pro Football Special Section, provided the coach was agreeable to it. Because I had a great relationship with Madden, he happily obliged (though he might have regretted it later). Our editors wanted Madden to burst through a large piece of paper for the cover, replicating what he did in the Miller Lite commercials, so one of our best photographers, Joey Ivansco, met me in California for the photo shoot at John's house in Danville. It turned out splendidly, but there was a point when Madden, after many takes and his back hurting from stooping down to burst through the paper, said politely but firmly that this next one would be the last.

No other newspaper or magazine had a pro football cover anywhere close to that cool and I was forever grateful to John for being so accommodating.

We never spoke about it all that often, but people always asked Madden about the famous "Immaculate Reception" AFC Divisional Playoff game against the Steelers in 1972, when Franco Harris miraculously caught a deflected pass at his shoe tops and raced to the end zone for a last-second TD to beat the Raiders.

The game, as you probably know, was always controversial. Many decades later, there are still Raider fans who insist the ball struck Steeler running back Frenchy Fuqua, not Oakland safety Jack Tatum (as was ruled), which would have disallowed Franco's catch under the rules back then.

However, following a frenzied conference with the entire officiating crew, Referee Fred Swearingen, after grabbing a dugout telephone and conferring upstairs with NFL Supervisor of Officials Art McNally, ruled the Pittsburgh touchdown to stand.

Madden always figured it went down something like this:

Swearingen: "Hey, if I call this Oakland's way, can you get a helicopter in here to take me out of the stadium?"

McNally: "No."

Swearingen, emerging from the dugout: "Touchdown, Pittsburgh!"

Nothing against the talents of Chuck Noll, but one thing is certain. Madden definitely would have been more fun.

CHAPTER 12

AL DAVIS

WHO WAS THE MOST INTERESTING, MOST INTRIGUING PERSON I ever covered?

No doubt, it was Al Davis.

Especially because of the Steelers-Raiders rivalry, the NFL's most hard-core rivalry of the '70s, and the attention it commanded. If you were reporting on this dynamic back then, you were mixing with Al Davis regularly. Without question, it was often bizarre and never boring.

You see, Al Davis had been called a genius around the NFL for so many years that he actually believed he was one. While he considered the Rooneys nice guys, I don't think he ever really respected them. Blue-collar guys from a dirty town, Al surmised, weren't about to prevail over him or the Raider organization, even if they did have a pretty smart coach, Chuck Noll, and had drafted all those future Hall of Famers.

So, whenever Al found an opportunity to spar with his main competition for Super Bowls, he was going to do it. And, if in the process it also involved the league and Commissioner Pete Rozelle, who did not hide his love for the Rooneys and their place in NFL history, all the better.

Therefore, it surprised nobody when:

Davis sued the Steelers and Noll for his "criminal element" comments regarding hits by defensive back George Atkinson on wide receiver Lynn Swann in both the 1975 AFC Championship Game and the 1976 season opener in Oakland.

Davis sued the NFL for blocking the Raiders' move from Oakland to Los Angeles.

When the Raiders played in Super Bowl XV in New Orleans, Al remained in his hotel room all week and, because of his feud with the NFL and Rozelle, stayed away from any typical Super Bowl week activities, only surfacing for the game.

After the traditional Friday Commissioner's press conference, when Rozelle referred to Al as "a charming rogue," Davis called Vito Stellino, my rival beat man, of the *Pittsburgh Post-Gazette* in his hotel room that afternoon and pronounced gleefully, "Boy, Pete played you guys like a bunch of violins."

I'm not going to lie to you. It was fun to write about Al Davis being the Darth Vader of the NFL, a line we often used. He always dressed in either black or white. His favorite outfit was a black leather jacket, white pants and shiny black loafers, gold eyeglass holders, and, of course, a gaudy Super Bowl ring.

Every once in a while Al would ditch the leather jacket and go with a black number that I liked to call "Dracula's golf sweater." Or show up in an all-black sweatsuit. Taking the hyperbole a bit further, we wrote about the apparent overly padded shoulders in Al's jacket and the alleged shoe lifts to make him look taller.

His affected "Southern accent" was usually assumed to have been created for recruiting purposes. Lord knows he didn't pick it up growing up in Brooklyn.

"Ah just want the RAY-duhs to be as great as we can be," Al would say in his unmistakable tone.

I went out to Oakland once to follow up on a story in *Sport* magazine, during which the Raiders' star quarterback, Kenny Stabler, who had a long feud with Davis toward the end of his career, said, "I'd like to bury the hatchet—right between Al Davis' shoulder blades."

Al wouldn't allow tape recorders in an interview because he didn't want any evidence, but I asked him if he seriously believed that Stabler would have made such a statement.

"People say a lot of things," Al said. "People write a lot of things. YOU write a lot of things."

"Like what?" I said.

"It's OK," Al said. "Ah understand."

"What do you mean?" I said.

"Do you really believe Ah wear lifts in my fuckin' shoes?" he said.

Vito and I were eating at an Oakland restaurant during a Steelers trip in 1976 and when it came time to pay the bill, the waiter told us it had been taken care of. We looked to our left and slightly over our shoulders, and there was Al, grinning and talking on a phone placed on his table. (This was a long time before cell phones, so phones on restaurant tables were highly unusual.)

"That's very nice, but you didn't have to do that," I told Al.

"Oh, Ah know," he said. "Ah wanted to."

I've had many people pick up dinner tabs for me, but when Al did it, you always expected to be making a return payment somewhere down the road. That, of course, is precisely why Al did it, to hold something over you. I don't say that unkindly. I liked Al for the most part and had tremendous respect for his football knowledge and his place in AFL/NFL history.

It's just a fact. Al was always playing the power game. On the field and off.

During the part of my career when I was spending a lot of time around Al Davis, I was rather proud of my impersonation of him. It might not have been as good as my Hubie Brown or my Rod Serling, but apparently, it was good enough to fool some people.

One year during training camp, Clark Judge of the *San Diego Union-Tribune* got me on the phone to do my Al Davis impersonation for a phony conference call with the Chargers writers, who were in on the charade.

Suddenly, Rick Smith, the long-time San Diego publicist, walked into the press room, heard what he figured was Al's voice, and said, "How the hell did you get him on the phone?"

It was at about that point that I totally lost it during the "interview" and Clark had to fess up about the charade.

I guess word never got back to Al about that one.

CHAPTER 13

THE FALCONS

WHILE A LOT OF THE STORIES AND ANECDOTES OF THIS chapter will have significantly more meaning for Atlantans, I think many of them will be entertaining even for those who haven't lived in the hub of the South.

I moved to Atlanta from Pittsburgh in the spring of 1979, with my then-wife Mary and our 3-month-old daughter, Jessica, convinced that it was the correct long-term career move for me, or at worst, a great transitional position for my next upgrade, working as the NFL and Falcons beat writer for the *Atlanta Constitution*.

As much as I loved Pittsburgh and its characters and covering the Steelers, it was still quite a dirty city back then and I was worried about raising kids in such a polluted industrial area. It's a far different place now with so many steel mills closed down, but in 1974, when I first moved there after college, a stench of orange sulfur dioxide filled the air every day. Sadly, Pittsburgh's famous three rivers were never going to be confused with Lake Tahoe.

Atlanta was clean, fresh, and new, with milder winters (though colder than the Chamber of Commerce likes to admit), roads without potholes, and tall Georgia pines against an azure sky. Although I missed Pittsburgh terribly in those early months and even pondered going back for a job with the *Post-Gazette*, I learned to love Atlanta as fondly as anywhere I had ever been—especially the northern suburbs of Roswell, Dunwoody, and Alpharetta.

Our second child, Katie, was born there in 1981, at Northside Hospital. Although Mary and I divorced in 1987, we made many great friends in Atlanta and owned several different homes. I ended up staying there for almost 40 years, just slightly longer than Nora, my bride of 1993, who had moved to Atlanta from Hilton Head, S.C., in 1980.

Although I covered the NFL nationally for the *AJC*, the Falcons initially were my main focus, and they were quite a different animal than the Steelers.

An expansion team that made its NFL debut only 13 years before I arrived, the Falcons and owner Rankin Smith, Sr. were a strange concoction.

They had a few top-quality offensive players, like quarterback Steve Bartkowski, who still had a gun to go with his sack-ravaged knees, or speedy receiver Alfred Jenkins and veteran center Jeff Van Note, but their main attraction was the undersized, over-achieving "Grits Blitz" defense that held opponents to a record 129 points in 1977. The Falcons made the playoffs the next year as a wild card and defeated Philadelphia, but then lost a divisional game to the Dallas Cowboys.

Which is when I entered the scene.

Coach Leeman Bennett always thought I was spoiled, having covered the Steelers during a couple of Super Bowl seasons, and maybe I was. But I came into the job with total objectivity, not expecting a similar result, and excited about fresh surroundings and new people.

That said, I wasn't ready for 6-10 that first year.

I thoroughly enjoyed Leeman, who actually posted a winning record (47-44-1) in six seasons but was abruptly fired by the Falcons after a playoff loss in the strike year of 1982. Landing his first head coaching job after four years as an LA Rams assistant, Bennett had no way of knowing that the Atlanta ownership would be so inept.

It's nothing less than a miracle that they occasionally hired talented outside front office people such as Eddie LeBaron, Ken Herock, or Bobby Beathard, and eventually promoted long-time personnel man Tom Braatz to general manager.

Rankin Smith, Jr., the eldest son, who would eventually become president when his father died, was clueless as an NFL executive and did nothing to disprove the notion that back then, as people often said, you could be accepted at the University of Georgia "with an expired fishing license." (It was much different in the 1990s when my daughters went to Georgia and a 1200-plus SAT was the norm.)

Since the Smiths were commonly referred to as The Clampetts, Rankin, Jr. naturally had to be our Jethro, and it was common to see his long, black Mercedes, with a bass boat trailing, pulling into his parking space at the Falcons Complex. Once I saw him carrying a 12-pack of Bud into his office and joked, "I see you brought your briefcase today, Jr."

He offered an awkward smile. I'm not sure he even understood the reference.

We never got along very well, largely because I regularly pointed out the Smith family's general ineptitude and he presumed the media's job was to support the team, not criticize it. But things went sharply downhill at a game in Kansas City in 1985.

I had finally reached my limit with Rankin, Jr.'s habit of sitting in the press box in the row behind the writers (not in the owner's suite, from where most NFL front office people watched the game) and regularly screaming at officials or Falcons players. His brother, Taylor, pro personnel man Bill Jobko and Braatz were usually there, too, but they mostly kept their comments to themselves.

Rankin, Jr., however, always liked to show off and on this day, I decided I wasn't going to accept it any longer. After all, he was sitting in "my office," the press box, and it wasn't acceptable to yell, "You choked, ref!" or to rip one of his players by asking, "Is that the best we've got?" On this day, when quarterback Dave Archer unloaded a wobbly pass, Rankin, Jr. could not help himself and made a "Ducks Unlimited" reference.

So, in addition to my game story that day, I wrote a sidebar on Rankin, Jr.'s antics, complete with the exact down and distance, plus the time on the game clock, when the remarks were uttered.

Naturally, Rankin, Jr. was furious and didn't talk to me for a year, which I didn't consider a bad thing. Most of his friends ridiculed him for his behavior, too, which was particularly nice to hear, summarizing it by saying, "Jr., you just got caught being Rankin, Jr."

I had no issues with Taylor, who was always pleasant and clearly the smartest of the family, or even Rankin, Sr., who never took himself too seriously and was a lot funnier than he knew. Plus, I was forever grateful for his offer to join him on his private jet to Steeler owner Art Rooney's wake in Pittsburgh.

We were in Tampa one year for a game against the Bucs and were staying at the Westshore Marriott near the airport. I went down for breakfast the day of the game and happened to notice Rankin, Sr. across the room at another table. While we weren't going to invite each other to dine, we pleasantly exchanged waves.

I sat at my table, which was close enough to hear Rankin, Sr. ordering his breakfast.

"I'll have two eggs, sunny side up," he told the waitress, "toast, and, uh......are the grits extra?

ARE THE GRITS EXTRA? ARE YOU KIDDING ME?

You're worth maybe $50 million and you're asking whether the grits are extra or come with the breakfast at no charge?

I was waiting for the waitress to say, "Yeah, they're a buck-25. You still want 'em?"

Rankin, Sr. was sitting in the owner's suite at Atlanta-Fulton County Stadium during one game when a plane buzzed the stadium with a sign trailing that said, "SELL THE TEAM, JED!"

Understandably unaware of the Clampett reference, his young granddaughter looked back and him and said, "Grandpa, I thought you owned the team!"

Until Home Depot co-founder Arthur Blank eventually bought the team in 2002, the Falcons' circus ran year-round.

Rankin, Jr. eventually was fallen by a couple of paternity suits, went through a divorce, and left the franchise, only to re-surface with a hair stylist in South Georgia.

The Falcons hired Dan Henning, the Redskins' highly touted offensive coordinator, in 1983 to replace Bennett. A talented offensive mind with an ego the size of his native Brooklyn, Henning never quite fit in with the folksy fans of the Deep South or the Smith family.

I don't want to say that Henning was short on class, but it kind of ran in the family. Even his daughter bummed cigarettes.

The Henning era was quite a contrast to the Falcons of the '70s. Back then they had a bunch of what were known as "God-Squad" players, led by linebacker Greg Brezina and safety Ray Easterling. I always thought they cheapened their religious beliefs by putting them so front and center—same as the victorious boxer who will give God top billing over his left hook—and even Leeman once said to me, "I never heard of God taking a team to the Super Bowl."

Once after a loss, Brezina looked at me and said, "Glenn, God understands why you write the things you write."

Instead of drifting away from his locker, I wanted to say, "Really? Then maybe he can tell me what to write tomorrow, Greg, because right now I'm clean out of ideas!"

One of my favorite Falcons players was Billy "White Shoes" Johnson, the dynamic return man from Houston who was added to the Atlanta roster in 1982. Not only did Billy provide loads of excitement in a Falcons uniform, but he was also the main character in a bizarre incident that occurred off the field.

A charitable guy with his time, Billy had started a promotion known as "The Day Santa Claus Wore White Shoes" and was to deliver toys to kids at Egleston Children's Hospital in Sandy Springs. It was a nice gesture, and I was on the scene, with a PR guy representing the sponsor, as Billy toured the hospital rooms in a red Santa Claus cap with a giant bag of toys flung over his shoulder.

Everything was going fine until a hospital employee, who brought along his child that day, said to the kid as Billy entered the room, "There he is. Don't you want to meet Johnnie Black Feet?"

I gulped and immediately swiveled toward Billy, thrilled to see no reaction. To this day, though, I don't know whether he didn't hear it or did hear it and decided to ignore it.

Either way, the PR guy nearly fainted.

"What a fan!" he said, moving to the next room.

The second head coach in Falcons history, the fiery Norm Van Brocklin, had been long gone from the scene by the time I arrived in Atlanta, but he was still a known figure, appearing regularly on a Turner Broadcasting NFL show and frequently seen around town.

As a coach, you might know that Van Brocklin feuded with running back Harmon Wages, AKA "Charmin' Harmon" from the University of Florida, and there's a famous NFL Films clip of the miked-up coach dressing down Wages on the sideline, treating him like a child.

Well, even at a Falcons golf tournament weekend in the mid-1980s, long after both men left the game, they exchanged words at a Penrod's cocktail party, and reportedly punches were thrown.

My editor told me to find Van Brocklin at the Atlanta Athletic Club the next day to report on the incident. I went reluctantly, feeling more like a supermarket tabloid reporter than a beat guy.

"Did you hit him, or did he hit you?" I asked Van Brocklin. "What started it? Is there still bad blood from the sideline incident?"

Answering none of my rapid-fire questions as he drew on a cigarette, Van Brocklin stopped me before I could deliver the next one.

"You're better than this, Sheeley," he decided.

Come to think of it, yes, I was.

It was probably fortunate that I didn't have to cover Van Brocklin as a player or coach. He raged against reporters throughout his career, maintaining his disdain for them even when faced with a brain operation in 1979.

"If I need a brain transplant," he said, "I hope I get one from a sportswriter because I want one that hasn't been used."

People tell me I should have been insulted by that quote. Sorry, but I'm not. It's just too good of a line.

CHAPTER 14

DON SHULA

ON SHULA, THE FAMED MIAMI DOLPHINS COACH, WAS ONE of my favorite people in the NFL. We enjoyed an exceptionally candid relationship, as I was able to kid him, even in a formal press conference situation, leading some of my fellow writers to occasionally gasp at my questions.

We got to know each other pretty well, first when the Dolphins spent several days practicing with the Atlanta Falcons at training camp in Suwanee, Ga., back in the mid-1980s, and twice-daily press conferences increased our familiarity with each other. Also, later when I was Pro Football Writers of America president in 1988-89, Shula served on the NFL Competition Committee with Tex Schramm of Dallas and was always addressing the media at NFL Owners Meetings, which were quite a plum to cover in warm weather sites in March.

We were at a press conference one day and, being the occasional smart-ass I was, I asked Shula if he figured that being on the committee might "help him with the officials," seeing as though the Dolphins were among the league's most penalized teams.

Arms crossed and stern-faced, at least for effect, Shula snapped, "Cut it out."

Even Shula's PR man, Chip Namius, didn't realize I could kid Shula in that manner and get away with it, and even said something to me afterward. I told him not to worry about it.

One day after practice with the Falcons, Shula met the press wearing a pair of those goofy white plastic sunglasses that were popular back then. At each corner was a little aqua Dolphin.

"What do you think?" Shula said, modeling the glasses.

"I think they'd look better," I said, "with a little blue Smurf at each corner."

"Fuck you," Shula said, smiling, and we all laughed.

During the 1980 NFL Owners Meetings in Honolulu, a sightseeing trip was planned for mid-week to visit Pearl Harbor. The NFL invited the attending media to join several head coaches for the trip, which was just a short ride from Waikiki Beach, where we were staying. In addition to Shula, on the bus were Forrest Gregg (Bengals), Bart Starr (Packers), and several other head coaches.

When we got to Pearl Harbor and the bus stopped, suddenly a very large Hawaiian man appeared in the doorway and announced, "I will be your guide today. My name is Manny Fernandez."

"WHAT!" Shula said, blown away that the guide would share the name of his famous Dolphins linebacker, halfway around the world.

Nobody won more NFL games than Don Shula or won more friends in the NFL. I miss him, the same as I do Arnold Palmer. Men like this are special and, unfortunately, a lot of people don't fully realize it until they're gone.

CHAPTER 15

DEION SANDERS

Stopping by Deion Sanders' Braves locker one day during that crazy time when he was playing for both the Falcons and Braves in the early '90s, I needed some quotes for a story I was writing that day for the *Atlanta Journal-Constitution*.

If there was one thing you could count on, it was that Prime Time's mouth would usually be moving as quickly as his feet.

But suddenly, he promptly informed me, "I ain't talking to no Glenn Shitley."

I had written many things about Deion during his stay in Atlanta—some that he obviously didn't think were as humorous as I felt they were.

Like when the Falcons drafted him No. 1 and there were discussions about what number he should wear.

I suggested the number from his arrest record on a battery charge at Florida State in 1988, although I wasn't sure it would fit on an NFL jersey.

I actually liked Deion's "Shitley" thing and so did my colleagues at the *AJC*, so much that they still fondly use the term on occasion.

But Deion never really did understand a reporter's job. And so, on this day, I decided to teach him a little about the profession.

"Let me ask you something, Deion," I said. "If I had a choice between being at home playing with my kids or standing here talking to you, where do you think I would be?"

Not even Deion's massive ego could allow that question to be misunderstood.

Deion and I had a much better relationship after that day.

CHAPTER 16

O.J. SIMPSON

I F YOU WERE A PRO FOOTBALL WRITER IN THE '80S AND EARLY '90s, you would regularly run into O.J. Simpson, who was working for NBC then, and showed up at practice facilities all around the NFL to do interviews or offer his observations.

I recall one day in the late '80s at Rams Park in Anaheim, Calif. While I was working on a story in the media area, O.J. grabbed one of the phones for media use behind me, became visibly agitated during the conversation, raised his voice a bit and finally slammed down the phone.

I always wondered if perchance he had been talking to his wife, Nicole, at that very moment. And if he was, what if I had walked over and said something like, "C'mon, Juice, it can't be that bad. I'm sure she loves you. Let it go."

Could history have been altered to where that infamous day in June of 1994 had never happened?

No, not likely, but I always thought about it.

Truth is, O.J. was a great NFL player to deal with and was always extremely friendly as a TV or movie guy. With the Buffalo Bills, I remember a game he played against the Steelers at Three Rivers Stadium in 1975. After a 227-yard rushing day that included an 88-yard touchdown run, O.J. was still at his locker speaking with reporters, still in full uniform, while most of his teammates were already showered, dressed, and heading to the team bus. That was typical O.J.

His arrest for the murder of Nicole Simpson and Ron Goldman came on June 17, 1994, which happened to be Friday of the U.S. Open at Oakmont Country Club near Pittsburgh. After the low-speed chase of O.J.'s white Ford Bronco on the 405 in LA, all the giant screens in the USGA press center for hours were showing the vehicle parked in the driveway of his Brentwood home. When we all departed for our hotel that night, it was nearly 10 p.m. Eastern time. Like everyone else, we feared O.J. would either shoot someone or be shot in his driveway at any moment.

Fortunately, that never happened.

The PGA Championship was at Riviera CC the next year, very close to Nicole's condo, and the media bus to the course each morning spent some time on Bundy Drive, the scene of the crime.

I will always remember seeing O.J.'s old locker in the Riviera clubhouse that week, closed off from the rest.

Such a horribly sad story, even now, almost 30 years later. Nobody will ever be able to separate O.J., the football player, from O.J., the presumed murderer. Nor should they.

CHAPTER 17

CANTON

WHEN I WAS COVERING THE NFL AND THE FALCONS FOR THE *AJC* in the '80s and '90s, I was honored to serve as president of the Pro Football Writers of America (PFWA) for 1987-88, following such prominent fellow writers as Edwin Pope of the *Miami Herald*, Paul Zimmerman of *Sports Illustrated*, Cooper Rollow of the *Chicago Tribune* (who had named me vice-president the year before) and my old Steelers beat rival, Vito Stellino.

Pro football writers back then were always fighting for player access and I was proud that during my time as president, we finally established a mandatory daily time where the locker room had to be open for the media. Although there were still teams whose players hid in the sauna during the locker room period or just vanished, the NFL enforced the access rule and teams were fined if they didn't cooperate.

My other contribution was starting an annual PFWA party at the Super Bowl, which, unfortunately, lasted only a couple of years, finally proving way too expensive. The NFL could hold theirs and spend millions, but ours cost $10,000 and whacked our budget for the year. Maybe we just weren't meant to be part of the social calendar. At least I tried.

Clearly, though, a few other duties that accompany the PFWA presidency were extremely exciting, regarding the Pro Football Hall of Fame, a place that until then I had not been fortunate enough to visit.

First off, during Hall of Fame week in Canton, Ohio, you are invited to a Saturday luncheon which is attended by every HOF member who happens to be attending the festivities that week. This means you go into a room where nearly every living NFL star you remember growing up is hanging around, holding a cocktail and telling stories. I don't recall everyone who was in there, but I do remember Joe Namath, Paul Hornung, Dick Butkus, and Johnny Unitas being among them. I was 36 at the time and still young enough to be blown away by such impressive company.

As PFWA president, you also have the honor of presenting the year's media entry into the HOF, the winner of the Dick McCann Award. In 1987 it was my pal, Jerry Magee, of the *San Diego Union-Tribune* who was going to be inducted.

When I flew into Canton that early August night in 1987 and was picked up at the airport by their long-time publicist, Don Smith, I had no idea of what I was getting into. I was told I'd be introducing Jerry at a luncheon and asked Don if I should prepare something to say. I figured it would be a little banquet room with a handful of tables.

"How many people are going to be there?" I asked Don.

"About 3,500," he said.

I just about fell out of the car. I immediately went to my room to prepare something hopefully witty enough to satisfy the occasion.

When I arrived the next morning and saw that the luncheon site was an arena, I certainly was glad to have some prepared remarks. I can't remember exactly what I said, but there were a few good lines, and I got some laughs.

On the way back to my seat, none other than Hank Stram, the famous Kansas City coach, hit me on the butt with a rolled-up program, just like the one he always carried on the sidelines.

"Good job, kid," Stram said, grinning.

As PFWA president, you also get to vote for which players get into the Hall of Fame that year. Up for consideration then was Miami Dolphins quarterback Bob Griese and somebody was arguing that we should induct him now before it was too late, as his wife was very ill.

Really? Nothing against Bob Griese and his wife's condition, but what the hell, I asked myself, did that have to do with his qualifications for making the Hall of Fame?

So, probably against my better judgment, seeing as though I was just a temporary voter and many of these writers had been there for decades, I decided to speak up.

"All due respect," I said, "but I don't remember hearing about an urgency to have Al Davis voted in when his wife was sick."

Well, you'd have thought I had endorsed Hitler. Heads swiveled around toward me and reading glasses were lowered onto noses. Although people mellowed significantly toward the Oakland Raiders' owner in later years, back then many considered him the NFL's Dr. Evil.

A month or so later, I was at an airport baggage claim one day and ran into Mike Ornstein, who was then working for Davis and the Raiders.

A suit bag draped over his shoulder, Ornstein reached out a hand and said, "Al heard what you did for him, and he appreciates it."

"I just said what I felt was right," I said.

"Well, if there's anything Al can ever do for you," Ornstein said, "he wants you to let him know."

Deciding that this sounded a little too mob-like for my comfort zone, I just nodded.

It was just Al being Al, most likely, but I never called to collect on his offer.

CHAPTER 18

PR GUYS

GREAT PUBLIC RELATIONS GUYS ARE HARD TO FIND WHEN you're a journalist. Too many of them don't understand your job. Too many of them who do understand it only care about keeping things they feel are negative out of the newspaper.

I was incredibly lucky. I dealt with many good PR guys throughout my career and many of them are still friends.

Maybe that's why I was able to switch to PR during the last part of my career and not feel like I was selling out.

I'm including a chapter on PR guys because they're such a big part of your life when you're covering a team or a league.

Seriously, during the NFL season, I probably spent more time with Joe Gordon of the Pittsburgh Steelers in the 1970s or the Atlanta Falcons' Charlie Dayton during the 1980s than I did with my wife.

Hmm, maybe that's why my first marriage didn't even last 10 years.

While Joe Gordon had to regularly deal with the hoopla that accompanied a Super Bowl champion team drawing national attention for many years, he had the much easier job, working for the best family in NFL history, the Rooneys, and being trusted to make wise decisions.

Conversely, Charlie Dayton had to navigate around the Smith family, which was not widely respected around the league, and a knee-jerk reaction franchise barely a dozen years old.

Can you imagine? Charlie was fired by the Falcons in 1987 because, according to management, he had "gotten too close to the media."

What a joke! Charlie was one of the best PR guys in NFL history and even has a press box named after him in Charlotte. Plus, he was once named to the All-Madden Team.

Chris Mortensen, who was also on the Falcons and NFL beat at the *AJC* before his days as an award-winning ESPN insider, Gerry Fraley and I had an understanding with Charlie. We asked that he tell us as much as he could, without jeopardizing management or players. It didn't usually involve providing information, but rather confirming or denying a story or letting us know if we were on the right track.

In return, whenever possible we would let Charlie know exactly what we were writing for the next day's paper so he wouldn't be surprised over his morning breakfast and without time to prepare his response to other media or Falcons management. And it worked out splendidly. We broke plenty of stories in the *AJC*, while Charlie kept things stable on his end and kept the Falcons in the news. Which, in the end, is the goal, isn't it?

If you require some additional evidence of Charlie's talents, consider that when he left the Falcons, he became publicity director for the Washington Redskins during their Super Bowl run, then moved to Carolina, where he became VP of Communications.

I barely had an angry word with either Joe or Charlie over the 15 years I dealt with them. They weren't always thrilled with what I was writing, but they usually understood why I was doing it. In turn, I usually understood why they were miffed at a story and why they sometimes had to make a statement questioning its accuracy or viewpoint.

There were many other PR guys I greatly respected, like the late John Morris, who was Sports Information Director at Penn State when I was a student and later worked for both the USGA and the PGA Tour; Ernie Accorsi, who became a renowned executive with the Browns, Colts, and Giants; Joe Browne of the NFL league office; or other NFL team PR guys such as Rick Smith with the Chargers and Rams, Jim Saccomano at Denver, and Jerry Walker with the 49ers.

In golf, I was also fortunate to work with Lee Patterson, Mark Mitchell, James Cramer, Phil Stambaugh, Joan Alexander, and Dave Lancer of the PGA Tour; Glenn Greenspan at Augusta National; David Fay of the USGA; Julius Mason with the PGA of America; Arnold Palmer's long-time publicist, Doc Giffin; Jack Nicklaus' guy, Scott Tolley; and my old friend John Marshall, who for many years handled PR for Atlanta's PGA Tour, LPGA Tour and Champions Tour events.

Many of these guys were former sportswriters, and I think that's important to remember. It's no coincidence that they were among the best PR guys, possessing not only a genuine news sense but also a true understanding of a reporter's job. Our first responsibility was to our editors and newspaper management, not the team or organization we were covering, and they were able to keep those facts in mind while also protecting their interests.

When I left the *AJC* in 2005 to work for The Golf Club of Georgia, suddenly my role was reversed. Instead of interviewing people, occasionally I was being interviewed to either promote our events or provide information.

Because I was unfamiliar with the role, there were even times when I asked someone who was interviewing me to read back a quote that I had just given them. I did that a few times for someone during a 35-year newspaper career, but certainly not often.

As I said, being on the other side of things put me in a hugely different position.

Instead of writing a PR release or tournament program piece for a million independent readers, now I was writing to present the Club in the best possible light. It's not lying or shading the truth. It's just avoiding things that reflect poorly on your company or emphasizing those things that create a positive image.

On one occasion at The Golf Club of Georgia in the early years of our United States Collegiate Championship, we learned that one of our caddies, employed to carry the bag for one of our college players that day, was going to be arrested by local authorities immediately after the round. As I recall, I believe it was for bouncing checks and the police were going to nab the guy right there off the 18th green.

But because we had a few media people covering the event, obviously this was a potentially negative situation for the Club. It was bound to overshadow anything that happened with our teams on the golf course that day if it became public knowledge.

As it turned out, only *Golfweek* and *Golfweek TV* were covering that day, including their long-time college golf writer, the late Ron Balicki, one of my best friends in the business and a huge promoter of the USCC. I wasn't worried about Ron. I knew I could pull him off to the side and explain the sensitivity of the development and he would treat us fairly. I wasn't so sure about his *Golfweek TV* partner, Asher Wildman, who was young, talented, and industrious and didn't know me very well, and his cameraman.

One thing was clear, I couldn't risk them seeing the arrest of a club employee during our biggest event.

So, to lure them away from the 18th green, which was just outside the media room, I suggested to the three of them that we take a visit to our TaylorMade Performance Center downstairs, a high-tech teaching bay with the latest swing analysis equipment. Sure, they said, and we went down to the basement for an hour or so, putting them all through the computerized TaylorMade teaching process.

Not only were they hugely impressed with the technology and feeling better about their golf swings, but by the time we got back upstairs, my PR world was under control. The caddie in question had finished his round, been handcuffed by the police, and taken off the property, with no media witnesses.

None of the three guys ever knew the real story about that day. My friend Ron Balicki is gone now, but if Asher happens to read this or finds it through a Google search, I expect a friendly call from him.

Hopefully, he'll chuckle about it and just give me points for PR creativity.

CHAPTER 19

THE ERNIE HOLMES TRIAL

I
T WAS THE STRANGEST BIG STORY I EVER COVERED AND ALSO ONE of the best.

It was February, 1977. Steelers defensive tackle Ernie (Fats) Holmes on trial in Amarillo, Tex., for possession of cocaine.

Steelers coach Chuck Noll, linebacker Andy Russell, and then vice-president Dan Rooney all appearing on his behalf.

A restroom constructed in the courtroom to help re-enact how Holmes, in town to attend a wedding, was approached by Metro Intelligence cops after purchasing a "silver bullet" (or cocaine snifter) for $20 while he was at the restroom urinal of the Rum Keg Lounge at the Howard Johnson's Motor Inn.

It was surreal.

We came back from lunch one day and carpenters were banging away, just finishing up the "restroom" model to illustrate exactly where everyone was standing when the arrest was made. They wouldn't allow the jurors to travel to the actual restroom, so they brought the restroom to them.

Just normal off-season stuff, right?

Yes, I guess so, when the guy on trial once shot at a police helicopter, wounding a cop, enjoyed shaving his head into an arrowhead, was known to wolf down a pack of cold hot dogs on his way to a game and almost singlehandedly stopped the Oakland Raiders in the 1974 AFC Championship Game, lifting the Steelers to their first Super Bowl.

Outside of any local Amarillo coverage, three newspaper reporters—myself for the *Pittsburgh Press*, Vito Stellino of the *Pittsburgh Post-Gazette*, and Randy Harvey, then of the *Dallas Times-Herald*—covered this bizarre event, along with Ray Kennedy of *Sports Illustrated*.

Now spending a week in Amarillo is one thing—in the space of three days we experienced an 82-mph sandstorm, 75-degree sunny conditions, and then a blanket of snow—but doing so in the middle of this zoo was something else.

On the stand, DA Tom Murphy asked Ernie about the shiny cylinder in question, which allegedly contained the drug.

"What did you think a 'silver bullet' was, Mr. Holmes?" Murphy said.

Replied Ernie, "I heard about silver bullets on the Lone Ranger."

Wide-eyed and his voice increasing in pitch, Murphy asked, "Mr. Holmes, did you think it was one of the Lone Ranger's silver bullets?"

"I didn't know what it was," Ernie said.

The DA asked him how much money he had with him.

Ernie said, "Twenty dollars and change."

The DA said, "So you gave this guy all the money you had?"

Ernie said, "I had more money back in my room at the Hilton."

The DA said, "Back there with the rest of your cocaine, isn't that right, Mr. Holmes?"

You couldn't make this stuff up. A DA with a 51-0 record for drug convictions. A Steeler defensive tackle who existed as an animal on the field and virtually a child everywhere else.

The story ended with Ernie being acquitted largely because the cops, who probably set him up, screwed up their stories under oath and contradicted each other.

The Sports Illustrated headline on Ray Kennedy's story read: "PITTSBURGH FATS DODGES A SILVER BULLET."

I filed seven pages of courtroom testimony about "silver bullets," the Lone Ranger, and cocaine, and the *Press*, while frequently clueless regarding other big national stories, ran every one of the nearly 2,000 words, starting it atop the front page and jumping it inside.

I often thought about what Ernie Holmes' life might have been like if convicted of a drug charge in Texas in the mid-1970s. I doubt the man would have ever survived prison. Despite the reprieve in Amarillo, Ernie spent only one more year in the NFL, traded by the Steelers in 1978 to Tampa Bay (cut in the preseason), and then playing three games with New England before retiring. His violent life ended at age 59 in 2008 from a single-car accident near Lumberton, Tex.

When Ernie had shaved his head into the shape of an arrowhead in 1974, he was asked by long-time Steelers publicist Joe Gordon, "What the hell did you do that for?"

According to the *Associated Press* obit of Jan. 18, 2008, Gordon said Ernie told him, "That's to point me to the quarterback."

In retrospect, a man who often appeared confused about the direction of his life probably needed the assistance.

CHAPTER 20

HUBIE BROWN

THE FACT THAT HUBIE BROWN IS STILL DOING NBA GAMES ON TV at 90 is nothing short of miraculous. If I'm flipping channels and hear his voice, I stop to watch the game, regardless of who is playing. I can't say that about any other announcer or analyst.

I feel very fortunate to have known Hubie in 1979-82 during the period when he was coaching the Atlanta Hawks. Although the NFL was my main beat then, I filled in for our *AJC* Hawks beat guys frequently or was sometimes added to our coverage as either a columnist or feature writer during the regular season and playoffs.

Hubie was the face of the Hawks back then. He was young, sometimes wild, and usually intimidating.

Yes, he cursed too much. You could hear it all over the arena and even on the TV broadcast. I always felt the habit tainted his image, and that's a shame.

And while there were players who didn't respond well to his screaming and profanity, usually Hubie Brown got more out of his players than anyone in the NBA; he knew more about basketball than most everyone else (and probably still does); and, of course, he was incredibly entertaining.

That said, Hubie was always disgusted by those NBA players who allowed themselves to destroy their bodies with drugs, especially the talented ones who still managed decent careers despite their altered states.

You might remember John Drew, who was a great scorer for the Hawks under Brown, but, unfortunately, also brought out the scoring in his opponents. Drew's defensive shortcomings were well known, and this was a constant irritation for Hubie, whose teams had traditionally been among the league defensive leaders. Adding to his ire, Drew was often injury-prone, slow-healing, and, in Hubie's opinion, a bit short on aptitude.

One day Hubie made an appearance at a Hawks booster club party, along with some media and Hawks players. While Hubie was chatting with a few boosters, he was approached by Drew, who despite the public setting, felt it was an appropriate time to assure the coach he could depend on him this upcoming season.

When Drew departed, Hubie decided to summarize the scene with the boosters by announcing, "There he is, John Drew. By far, the biggest (pussy) in the NBA."

If you remember when people used to have phone answering machines back in the '80s and '90s, I once set up mine with my best Hubie Brown impersonation, which at that time was pretty good.

The message said:

"(BEEP) Hi, this is Hubie Brown. Glenn is not home right now, but unless you are John Drew and unable to operate a phone, please leave your message at the tone and Glenn will get back to you as soon as he can."

I got a lot of laughs from my friends who heard it, but after a month or so, I took it down because of confusion that arose when, say, a bank or doctor's office might have called me.

Good thing, too. Two weeks later, Hubie called me back on my home phone. As much as I considered us friends, that might have been a bit awkward.

One year I took over for our beat guy on a lengthy West Coast trip made necessary by a Ringling Bros. Circus appearance at the Omni (then the Hawks' home). By this point in the season, NBA beat guys already were getting travel-weary, but for me, a long West Coast trip (maybe eight cities in 11 nights) was kind of fun.

(You've heard people say they travel so much that sometimes they must check the dial on the hotel phone to see what city they are waking up in? Well, this was one of those trips. If I remember correctly, it started in Denver, then Utah, Oakland, Portland, Seattle, LA, Chicago, and finally finishing in Detroit.)

Back then Utah was still playing in the old Salt Palace in Salt Lake City and, don't ask me how I remember, the refs that night were Mike Mathis and Paul Mihalik. The game had barely started when they called "traveling" on the Hawks.

Hubie exploded off the bench and screamed at them, chin classically tilted up and palms turned up at waist level.

"I don't know what the fuck it is with you guys!" Hubie bellowed. "Every time we play, you come in with a fucking hard-on!"

I turned around from the press table to the crowd, which was probably mostly Mormon, and saw nothing but shocked faces.

On that same trip, we were staying at the Edgewater Hyatt House in Oakland, Calif., waiting on the team bus to go to practice. Everybody was on the bus except, you guessed it, Drew. After a few minutes with the bus idling, the coach told equipment manager Joe O'Toole to call Drew's room.

A minute or two later, Joe returned to the bus to inform Hubie that Drew's telephone line was "busy," which, of course, was worse than not answering at all.

When Drew finally appeared and walked toward the bus steps, he was limping a bit and got a serious glare from Hubie, who always sat in the front aisle seat closest to the door.

Hubie had arranged an odd practice site for the day, a Mormon church in the Berkeley Hills, and when the bus finally came to a stop there, Hubie announced from his seat, turning back toward the players.

"OK, they are letting us practice here today, but there are two rules. You must keep your shirts on and there will be no swearing."

Darrell Simmons, who was covering for the *Atlanta Journal*, and I looked at each other and rolled our eyes.

When we got off the bus, a nearby gardener froze, stopping his hedge pruning as he stared at this line of very tall black guys filing past him.

It was at this point that Dan Roundfield, a 6-9 power-forward, said in his deep voice to the gardener, "Don't worry. We ain't stayin.'"

Inside the gym, the Hawks were warming up when Hubie commanded them to hold the balls and listen up.

In his typically booming voice, Hubie asked, "DO YOU KNOW HOW BAD YOU FUCKING SUCKED LAST NIGHT?"

Darrell and I looked at our watches. Hubie's no-swearing decree was already in shreds.

I decided to see Hubie speak to a high school group once, basically just to see if he could actually turn off the F-bombs when he had to.

And much to my surprise, he did. The talk was clean. The only slippage within the school's walls came before the speech. I asked

Hubie if he was going to grab a quick bite to eat in the high school cafeteria.

"Are you kidding?" he said. "Nobody can eat this fucking garbage!"

Although Hubie often left us shaking our heads at his tirades and loose language, he was a blast to be around.

When the Hawks fired him in 1982, they were too intimidated to do it in person and hid behind the safety of a speakerphone from West Palm Beach, Fla., where the Turner brass had assembled for spring training. When the press release of Hubie's firing was released by Hawks PR guy Chet Wright, it was handwritten and distributed to the media on, I kid you not, a piece of legal pad paper, complete with hurriedly scrawled cross-outs and inserts. I'd never seen anything so unprofessional.

My old *Atlanta Journal* friend and colleague, the late Dick Williams, who knew Hubie well, told me he went out to dinner with the Browns and the Mike Fratellos in New York shortly after Hubie took the Knicks job in 1982.

"So how's everything going?" Dick asked the coach.

"I've got three fucking free-basers," Hubie said, pretty much ending the dinner table small talk.

I'm certain that's one of the main reasons that TV always has been so appealing to Hubie. He can be around the game, make great money, and get his opinions and observations out there without a player's personal habits driving him nuts.

I hope he's behind the microphone for at least a little while longer. The NBA is bleeping better for it.

CHAPTER 21

MICKEY MANTLE

Y OU GET TO MEET YOUR BOYHOOD HEROES WHEN YOU WRITE about sports for a living. Sometimes it's a kick. Sometimes it makes you cringe.

When I was a Little Leaguer playing third base, I'd pretend I was Eddie Mathews of the Milwaukee Braves, scooping up a hot grounder and firing it to first base.

Then 30 years later, I saw Eddie Mathews signing autographs at a baseball card show with a pint of booze next to his chair, in a paper bag.

I had watched Yogi Berra on our black-and-white TV with the Yankees in World Series games of the late '50s and early '60s and then met him as the National League All-Star manager in 1974 in Pittsburgh when I had just started with the *Pittsburgh Press*. When I asked Yogi, standing there in long johns, whether he would have liked the Pirates' Richie Zisk, who had been unfairly snubbed, on his team, he scratched his balls and replied, "Shit, yeah!"

So much for idols.

The Mickey Mantle experience was a little different. While

disappointed that every kid's baseball hero, whom I met in Georgia when he turned 60, drank way too much, openly cheated on his wife, and could be so rude to people, the experience still maintained a certain glow.

In other words, despite all of this, it was still MICKEY FREAKIN' MANTLE!!

Yes, you give the most famous baseball player of your lifetime a little bit of slack.

When Jane Leavy was writing her Mantle book, *The Last Boy*, in 2010, she asked me to recollect a story that I had once shared with our mutual pal, Dave Kindred. It involved Mantle playing a round of golf at The Harbor Club in Greensboro, Ga., which he had adopted as a second retirement home away from Texas in the early 1990s, with Whitey Ford also in the group that day.

On the second hole, an elevated par-4 which plays to a green surrounded by water, with a small brick wall, Mantle tried a succession of misguided approach shots—one in the woods, one in the water, and one over the green—before finally getting a ball to remain on the putting surface. Trudging up to the green, Mantle chose not to walk around the low wall and instead decided to hoist himself over it, apparently forgetting that his knees were nearly shot. Losing his balance halfway over the wall, the guy who replaced Joe DiMaggio fell backward into the mud and water. With Ford and others rushing over to him, asking if he was all right, Mickey just looked up with that goofy Oklahoma grin and pronounced, "Tough fuckin' hole!"

When I spoke to Mickey in 1992 during a charity golf tournament at The Harbor Club, where the owners built a small museum filled with Mantle memorabilia, he mentioned that a writer from Fort Worth had asked him recently what he figured he'd be making if he was playing today.

"Oh, probably about $500,000," Mantle told him.

When the flabbergasted reporter informed Mantle that players are making $7 million or so a year these days, Mickey deadpanned, "Yeah, but I'm 60 years old."

When Mantle relayed the story to me, I said, "Somehow, I don't think I'm the first guy you used that line on."

Mantle grinned and took another sip from his beer.

He became quite a Braves fan in those days, being just down the road from Atlanta when the team made its famous turnaround and then dominated for more than a decade. He offered to throw out the first ball at a Braves game some night, but never got around to scheduling it with the front office. Not even with his ex-teammate, Bobby Cox, managing the Braves then.

Considering all the famous athletes I met over the years, with nobody else did I experience this strange feeling of excitement and sadness all at the same time, as I did with Mickey Mantle. There was not much depth to Mantle, the man, and it showed.

It wasn't the same as sitting across a lunch table with Arnold Palmer, noticing the two hearing aids, and feeling sad about witnessing his natural deterioration. Or watching Jack Nicklaus hobbling for his ceremonial tee shot at the Masters at age 80. Mantle's plight was different and voluntary. He had destroyed years of his baseball life by drinking and carousing to extremes and ignoring the warning signs of a declining body.

Sitting across from Mantle that first time, I found myself thinking back to 1961 when I was 10 years old. He and Roger Maris were in the middle of the most famous home-run race in baseball history and my parents had taken our family on an end-of-summer trip to Cooperstown, NY, to the Baseball Hall of Fame. All over town, they were keeping track of the HR totals between the two sluggers. I remember noticing the up-to-date numbers in scrawled paper signs taped to the inside of store windows.

Earlier that same season, attending a day-night doubleheader in Baltimore in mid-July with my dad, Mantle hit HR No. 32 to help win the first game against the Orioles. But when a storm hit with the second game only one out from being official and was rained out, Mantle lost HR No. 33 and Maris lost No. 36.

As most baseball fans know, while Maris eventually hit 61 homers over 162 games of the 1961 season, back then record keepers were distinguishing between Babe Ruth's 154-game season and the current 162-game schedule. So, for 154 games, Maris had fallen one short at 59 (in Baltimore, ironically), and I always thought about the rained-out homer we saw in Baltimore that would have tied Ruth's famous record.

When I met Mantle for the first time in 1992, this was the sadness I felt. A couple of anecdotes or stories into the conversation, I quickly realized he remained that same Oklahoma country boy, but now in a broken-down body, never forced to deepen his life beyond baseball, booze, last calls, and loose women.

Mantle knew it, too. When his body finally gave out, forcing him to leave baseball and the social life it created for him, he was virtually rudderless.

"After I retired in the spring of '69," he told me, "it was like Mickey Mantle died... I tried a bowling alley and a fast-food deal called Mickey Mantle's Country Chicken. Remember that? Our slogan was, 'To get a better piece of chicken, you'd have to be a rooster.'"

Strangely, there was still a shyness then to Mantle before he knew his liver was dying and that a transplant would be needed only three years later. Out of baseball for more than two decades then, he went from trying to avoid publicity as a New York Yankee to appreciating the occasional celebrity recognition as a part-time Greensboro, Ga., resident, playing golf or hanging out at Hug's bar with a regular group of friends.

"I'll tell you," Mantle said, "it's flattering as hell. The other day we had this (card) show in Memphis and this guy in overalls and no socks comes up with a little boy on his arm. He said, 'Mickey, you've been my idol all my life. I just want to thank you so much for making my life what it is.'

"Then he says to his kid, 'Son, this is Mickey Mantle. He's the greatest baseball player ever.' The little boy looked up at me and said, 'Daddy, he's an old man!'"

Laughing, Mantle said, "I thought the father was going to drop over."

Mickey Mantle died in 1995, two months and five days after his liver transplant. He was 63.

Sure, I'm glad I was fortunate to meet him, but I often wish it had been different.

The guy in my black-and-white TV back then seemed a lot cooler.

CHAPTER 22

STAN THE MAN

I NEVER REALLY KNEW STAN MUSIAL EXCEPT TO SAY HELLO TO him a few times at Cardinals games over the years at Busch Stadium.

Every kid back then knew who "Stan the Man" was, but being a Pennsylvania guy, I also knew he was from Donora, which was not that far from Pittsburgh, where I lived from 1974-1979 while working for the *Press*.

In 1982, though, when I was working for the *Atlanta Journal-Constitution*, he truly became "The Man" for me and many of my colleagues.

We were all covering the Braves-Cardinals Divisional Playoff that year, and the series schedule was altered by a rainout in St. Louis. As a result, everyone's flight arrangements back to Atlanta had been thrown into chaos.

So, to accommodate everyone, the National League organized a chartered media jet from St. Louis to Atlanta for Game 3.

This was wonderful news until everyone got to the airport that night and noticed our jet parked on the tarmac.

It was from Ozark Airlines, which for a while seemed to be dropping planes out of the sky at an alarming rate.

What a price for convenience! Well, at least, I will go down with my drinking buddies.

As we slowly took our seats, the fatalistic comments were coming from everywhere. Then suddenly we glanced toward the front of the plane. There he was, deeply tanned in a light beige suit, just boarding.

Stan the Man Musial.

Mr. Cardinal.

On our plane. The most cherished sports icon in St. Louis history, walking down the aisle and taking a seat in first class.

Surely, The Man Upstairs would protect The Man down here.

And all of us along with him.

Which is how it all turned out, of course, or else I wouldn't be writing this.

CHAPTER 23

TED, BOBBY & THE BRAVES

I'M GUESSING THAT YOU (OR YOUR PARENTS) MIGHT HAVE BEEN watching on national TV in 1977 when Ted Turner, the famous Atlanta sports owner, and television pioneer, slumped drunkenly under a table during the trophy presentation for the America's Cup race he had just won.

This is about the time when the nickname "Captain Outrageous" was born.

For those of us who were lucky enough to be in hearing range of Ted Turner in the '80s and '90s, chronicling his bizarre moves and quotes on an almost daily basis, this behavior was, well, fairly normal.

Ted Turner would do anything or say anything, at any time. Outrageous as it might have been, it usually was just to either have fun, seek attention, or both, and it was usually harmless.

If you saw Ted walking slowly enough through the press box to answer a few questions, you were wise to have an empty notebook or extra tape for your recorder on hand, because the man was likely to fill it.

My experience with the Ted Turner circus began even before I came to Atlanta to work for the *Atlanta Journal-Constitution* in 1979.

I happened to be writing a feature story for the *Pittsburgh Press* on the night of May 11, 1977, at Three Rivers Stadium, when Ted, having just fired manager Dave Bristol, decided he would manage the Braves until a replacement was found.

As it turned out, Ted's managerial act would be a one-night stand.

I was among a few reporters in the visiting manager's office as Ted, wearing the Braves' old light blue road uniform with his name across the back, was on the phone before the game with National League president Chub Feeney. Turner's feet and a pair of royal blue running shoes were up on the desk. He looked, well, quite comfortable.

Don't get used to this, Feeney explained. For the following night's game, Turner was told, he would have to designate someone other than himself to sit in the dugout.

Which he did. After Turner lost his game, 2-1, third-base coach Vern Benson took over the next night and won, ending the Braves' 16-game losing streak. For the next game, Bristol was given his job back for the remainder of the season.

Somehow that seems fitting, I guess. After so many wretched seasons before the Braves found success, what better indicator could there be than their owner with a winless record as manager?

If I ever needed Ted for a story—when he wasn't roaming the press box—he was usually good about getting on the phone, but he preferred to do it while wandering around his office via his speaker-phone, multitasking before there was a name for it.

This made for a strange type of interview as Ted would move to different areas of his spacious office, his voice fading when he stopped in a corner too far away from the phone, then blaring when he moved back toward the speaker.

I'll never forget the sign in the stadium tunnel, just down from the Braves' dressing room door, where Turner's car could usually be found. "DON'T EVEN THINK OF PARKING HERE!" the sign commanded.

When Ted married Jane Fonda in 1991, that's when he took on star status nationally. Yes, the guy was kind of crazy and he actually thought the country had an appetite for 24-hour news (before anyone else thought of it, of course), but marrying a big-time actress, that was something else again.

When the Braves managed their worst-to-first story in the early 1990s, Ted's box at Atlanta-Fulton County Stadium was quite the showcase. One night it might be Bill Murray joining him and Jane for a Braves game. On many nights it was Jimmy and Rosalyn Carter. Or maybe Halle Berry, who was dating David Justice at the time.

The Divisional Playoff or National League Championship Series post-game parties during those years were as tough of a ticket as the game. Turner's spread always featured the best of everything, including mountains of massive fresh shrimp scattered around the Stadium Club. While I couldn't always find a game ticket for Nora, if I got her into the post-game party, that was as good or better.

When the series switched to Philadelphia in 1993 for the NLCS, the mounds of beef for Philly Cheese Steaks offered by the Phillies brass looked like dorm food in comparison.

And with all of this happening, humble Bobby Cox first served as Ted's general manager, coming over from Toronto, and then his manager, taking his team to one of the most incredible stretches in baseball history with 14 straight division titles. Beyond that, Bobby was liked by absolutely everyone—even the umpires who saw his jaw up close for 162 ejections over 33 seasons.

Bobby Cox is one of the classiest men I ever met in sports, and it was a privilege just to have been around him for a few years. I loved sitting in the dugout with him before the games, often talking baseball, but sometimes not. Bobby just liked people, period, and he wanted to know about your newspaper editors, your family, or your colleagues in the press box.

However, he didn't always read the *AJC* as closely as I figured, which is probably a good thing for a nice-guy manager who might take things personally. Once I made the mistake of approaching Bobby before a game one day and apologizing for something very delicate that I didn't want to write in the previous day's paper but felt I had to.

"I didn't see it," Bobby said. "What did you write?"

Oops. Now I had to tell him. He was OK with it, but I would have rather the conversation had not taken place.

In 1993, I was doing national baseball for the *AJC* and spent a good deal of time at Braves spring training in West Palm Beach and touring other camps in Florida. This also meant working with our Braves beat writer, I.J. Rosenberg, whose personality and reporting style made him popular with editors, but not so much with his colleagues and many players. I prefer people who are humble and understated, which is why I eventually turned to golf, and though I.J. was very successful, he was neither of those things.

I was out in the Braves bullpen with Bobby one day, a few days into my stay at spring training in 1993, when the affable manager, out of nowhere, asked me, "So, how are you and the asshole getting along?"

I'm not sure what I answered, but I knew immediately to whom he was referring.

When I was doing PR and membership for both The Golf Club of Georgia and Hawks Ridge Golf Club after leaving the newspaper business, I was fortunate to spend time with members John Smoltz, Chipper Jones, and Tom Glavine. I've been around a lot of baseball players over the years, and I never heard any of them speak so lovingly about a manager as these guys did—and not just because he allowed them to take their golf clubs on road trips. It was a genuine affection, almost like sons to a father.

I could go several years without seeing Bobby, which I did after going into the golf business, and then bump into him at a cocktail reception and get a smiling response as though we were just sitting in the dugout together the day before.

"Hey, Glenn, how the hell are you?" Bobby would say.

I haven't seen him since his stroke in 2019, but I know when I do, it will be no different.

CHAPTER 24

TOMMY LASORDA

ODGERS MANAGER TOMMY LASORDA, AFTER A BRAVES GAME, with several writers hanging around in the locker room awaiting players returning from showers to speak with them, presented a distasteful vision that remains in my head to this day.

Here was Lasorda, quite naked (and this was not a good body, my friends), jiggling and prowling around the post-game buffet, holding only a fork and intermittently jabbing it into cold cuts or twirling some spaghetti.

"Pretty fuckin' good," he decided, glancing back at us.

Most of us decided right then to pass if someone handed us a plate and invited us to partake.

On another occasion, I was in Lasorda's office following a lopsided loss to the Braves, clustered around his desk with maybe a dozen other writers, the majority of whom were Dodger beat guys from LA.

We all watched silently as Tommy reached his hands into a giant metal bowl filled with Caesar salad and mixed it thoroughly. With his just-from-the-dugout hands dripping in oil and crouton crumbs, he grabbed a nearby bath towel, wiped off his hands, and started digging into the salad.

All the while, nobody is saying anything, not wishing to offer the first question, which had a very good chance of being answered with at least one expletive.

As Tommy stuffed salad in his mouth, Ken "Mouse" Gurnick of the *LA Herald Examiner* decided to leave, unable to deal with it any longer.

"Well, thanks for fuckin' stopping by, Mouse," Lasorda said.

I left shortly thereafter.

To this day, I'm not sure if anyone ever asked a question.

Terry Bradshaw of FOX Sports interviewing Philadelphia's Jalen Hurts after the NFC Championship Game, Jan. 29, 2023.

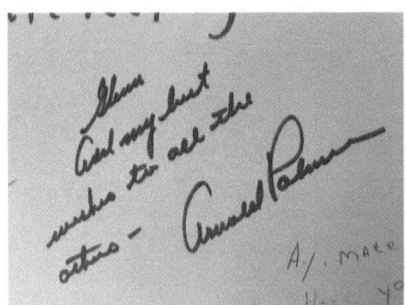

My fellow sportswriters at Bay Hill sent me a giant get-well card after my kidney cancer surgery in 1998, with Arnold Palmer's famous signature and good wishes squarely in the middle.

My first wife, Mary, and I with the late Steelers owner, Art
Rooney, Sr., at our wedding in 1977.

April 11, 1999

This letter authorizes <u>Glenn Sheeley</u> to play golf at the Augusta National Golf Club on Monday, April 12, 1999, at <u>8:52</u> A.M. You will play off the <u>10th Tee</u>.

Please present this letter at the gate for entrance to the Club grounds <u>and</u> at the tee.

James H. Armstrong, Jr.
General Manager

The letter officially allowing me to play golf at Augusta National the Monday after the 1999 Masters.

Myron Cope's famous "Terrible Towel"
has earned millions for the Autism Society
of Pittsburgh and the Allegheny Valley
School, where his son, Danny, attended.
(Photo Courtesy Autism Society of Pittsburgh)

Our beloved *Atlanta Journal*
columnist, the late Furman Bisher,
preparing to cover another major.
*(Photo Courtesy Golf Writers
Association of America)*

Interviewing Pete Rozelle, the late NFL Commissioner,
before a game in Atlanta in the 1980s. *(Walter Victor photo)*

With golf great Billy Casper, who served as Honorary
Captain for the 2013 Georgia Cup match.

With my late Pittsburgh newspaper pals, Dave
Ailes (left) and Phil Musick, at Phil's 65th
birthday celebration in 2003.

After breaking his ankle late in 1992, Greg Olson missed the World
Series, but sat down with me for a diary in the *AJC*.
(*Walter Victor photo*)

Handing out a Golf Writers Association of America award at
Augusta to former LPGA Commissioner Charley Meachem.
(Photo Courtesy Golf Writers Association of America)

With the late Atlanta Falcons owner, Rankin Smith, Sr., on the practice field at training camp in Suwanee, Ga.

Interviewing former NFL Commissioner Paul Tagliabue
before a game in Atlanta in the 1990's.
(Walter Victor photo)

With Tiger Woods, the new Masters champion, at the IMG media summit at Bay Hill in December 1997.

With Scott Van Pelt, then a broadcaster
for the Golf Channel, on the Monday after
the 1999 Masters, when we both played
Augusta National.

Standing on the Hogan Bridge on my way to
playing the famous par-3 12th hole at Augusta
National in 1999. Miraculously, I got up-and-down
for par from the back bunker.
(Sam Greenwood photo)

Presenting the Pro Football Writers of America's George S. Halas Award to Falcons running back William Andrews at Atlanta-Fulton County Stadium in 1987 for coming back from a career-threatening knee injury.

Hershey Country Club pro Jay
Weitzel (left), with Boston Celtics
great Bob Cousy at HCC, circa 1970.
(Photo Courtesy Hershey Country Club/
Jay Weitzel/Jim Reed)

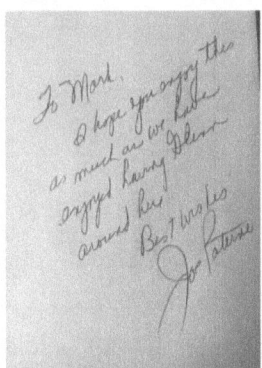

Joe Paterno's inscription in
my Dad's copy of *Football
My Way,* which was quite a
compliment to me.

Mickey Mantle signing an autograph at
the Harbor Club in Greensboro, Ga.,
about the time he turned 60.
(Photo Courtesy Jerry Grillo)

With my daughter Jessica on her
30th birthday in 2009, holding the
revised *Pittsburgh Press* front page
from the Steelers' victory in Super
Bowl XIII, just hours before her
birth, Jan. 22, 1979.

Jack Nicklaus

February 3, 1999

Dear Glenn:

Now that I'm back from Boston with my new hip, I wanted to thank you for the nice arrangement of flowers that you sent me during my stay at New England Baptist Hospital last week. The roses, daisies, lilies and snapdragons brought a little bit of spring to the room, even though it was snowing outside at times. It was great to receive such a welcome reminder that friends were thinking of us.

I know that I have my work cut out for me over the next few months as I rehabilitate, but I'm delighted with the results of the surgery and looking forward to getting back out on the golf course as soon as my progress will permit.

Thanks again.

Best regards,

Mr. Glenn Sheeley
Atlanta, GA 30341

/mk

The letter from Jack Nicklaus, thanking me for the flowers I sent him after his hip surgery in 1999.

Spending so many days on the road covering sports throughout my career, I missed a lot of time with these two beautiful girls, my daughters, Jessica (left) and Katie.

Nora and I at St. Andrews, Scotland, before my round there in 1999, the day after the Open Championship at Carnoustie.

My wife and I with actress Jane Seymour,
our special guest, at Nora's former store in
Roswell, Ga., Elegant Attic.

A dinner at Christopher's in Pittsburgh in the late '70s, with (left to right)
TV personalities Sam Nover and Yvonne Forston, myself, Dan Rooney,
Andy Russell, Rocky Bleier and restaurant owner Chris Passodellis.

PITTSBURGH STEELERS
300 STADIUM CIRCLE
PITTSBURGH, PA. 15212
412/323-1200

EXECUTIVE OFFICE

April 10, 1979

Mr. Glenn Sheeley

Pittsburgh PA   15221

Dear Glenn:

I hope you, Mary and Baby are well.

I just heard you are leaving the Press going to
the Atlanta Constitution. We'll miss you -- you
did a fine job for the Pittsburgh Press, the
fans, Pro football and the Pittsburgh Steelers.
You are very knowledgable.

I hope that you will be very happy in Atlanta.
We will always be happy to see you.

Good wishes always to you and yours.

Sincerely,

Art Rooney

**This letter sent to me by Art Rooney, Sr., a few weeks before I left
Pittsburgh for Atlanta, is one of my favorites.**

My good friend Shelby Strother, who
died in 1991 of liver cancer at only 44,
was a writing genius.
(*Courtesy Shelby Strother Family*)

With James Keach, who played the motorcycle cop famously
confronting Chevy Chase in the *Vacation* movie. James was Jane
Seymour's husband at the time and joined her for a reception at my
wife's store in Roswell, Ga., in January, 2007.

My first appearance on Golf
Channel's live *Viewer's Forum* show in
1997, hosted by Peter Kessler, whose
knowledge was unmatched. *(Courtesy
of Golf Channel)*

Sharing the couch on a later Golf
Channel *Viewer's Forum* show, with
Charles Davis and the late Tim
Rosaforte.
(Courtesy of Golf Channel)

A young Rich Lerner calling in live
from Houston to the *Viewer's Forum*
show in Orlando, with host Peter
Kessler and myself.
(Courtesy of Golf Channel)

On the set for taping of the CNN/
SI *Golf Plus* show, which sometimes
aired on CNN International and
could be seen worldwide.
(Screenshot/Video Capture of CNN)

Kyra Phillips hosting one of our *Golf Plus*
shows on CNN/SI, where I appeared
regularly as the PGA Tour insider.
(Screenshot/Video Capture of CNN)

Taping *Golf Plus* in the CNN studios in Atlanta,
with frequent host Bob Fiscella, getting my
take on PGA Tour news and events. *(Screenshot/
Video Capture of CNN)*

With John Madden in August 1986, at Riviera Country Club,
near LA, where he was playing in Raiders Coach Tom Flores'
charity golf tournament the day before we drove to John's home
in Danville, Calif., for an *Atlanta Journal-Constitution* story I was
doing. The five-hour trip with the Hall of Fame coach and TV's
most popular NFL analyst ever was a career highlight.
(Special)

CHAPTER 25

WHITEY HERZOG

OUTSIDE THE ST. LOUIS CARDINALS LOCKER ROOM AFTER A game with the Braves in the 1980s, I was standing next to long-time Atlanta sports radio guy Joe Walker, who is blind, when Manager Whitey Herzog approached.

Recognizing the manager's distinctive voice, Joe perked up and said, "Whitey, Whitey, I couldn't go a year without seeing you."

"Seeing me?" Herzog said, laughing. "Joe, you ain't seen anybody your whole fuckin' life."

"Yeah, Whitey," Joe said, "I know it, and I love you for sayin' it."

When Vince Coleman was stealing bases so amazingly for the Cardinals in the 1980s, the *AJC's* Executive Sports Editor, Van McKenzie, wanted to run a graphic in the paper depicting how long it took Coleman to get to second base.

"Go ask Whitey," Van said.

So, I drove over to the stadium for the game that night and asked the Cardinals manager during batting practice.

"How the fuck would I know?" Whitey said.

I said, "Well, then could you take a guess?"

"OK, three seconds," Whitey said.

I told this to Van, and he said, "We can't use three seconds. People will think we made it up... Let's use 3.2 seconds."

In other words, so Van made it up, anyway.

Lesson learned: Just because you are an expert in newspaper graphics, it doesn't mean you're a journalist.

CHAPTER 26

HUMAN ERROR

WHILE MY GOAL WITH THIS BOOK HAS ALWAYS BEEN TO entertain you, I wanted to mention a couple of incidents that have been on my mind since early in my career. Sadly, they are more disappointing than entertaining, yet they are extremely important to me and demonstrate the imperfections of the newspaper business, even decades ago, when it was strong, influential, and not yet competing with the internet.

Human decisions are still the final word, and sometimes they are so obviously the wrong ones.

Although both incidents happened at the *Pittsburgh Press*, where I have so many wonderful memories, they were impossible decisions to defend, and I think you will agree.

I was working at the *Press* when the Three Mile Island nuclear accident happened in Middletown, Pa., on March 28, 1979, just a 2 ½ hour drive from Pittsburgh, in Central Pennsylvania.

For those of you less familiar with the tragedy, there were major concerns that if the leak from the damaged reactor was not halted, the earth's core could have melted.

Yes, I said, THE EARTH'S CORE COULD HAVE MELTED!!

In other words, a big deal.

So, with this horrific thought in mind, what did *Press* Managing Editor Leo Koeberlein decide to do when the story broke?

To not send one of his reporters, is what he decided.

"It's a one-day story," he said. "Let the wires handle it."

Wow.

That next day, the *Pittsburgh Press* ran a front-page story about the Three Mile Island accident, plus a photo—from the Los Angeles Times. For a newspaper during these times, this was the ultimate embarrassment with a story so close to home and so huge.

And, by the way, the environmental clean-up from the "one-day story" took 12 years to complete and cost more than $1.5 billion.

On Nov. 27, 1978, I was in San Francisco awaiting the Steelers' Monday night game against the 49ers in old Candlestick Park.

We were paying our breakfast bill that Monday morning at the Edgewater Hyatt House in Oakland when we heard somebody say, "Oh, my god, they shot the mayor!?"

That was San Francisco mayor George Moscone, killed along with Supervisor Harvey Milk, by fellow Supervisor Dan White, a former cop.

Knowing the impact of the story, along with *Press* columnist Roy McHugh, plus Phil Musick and Vito Stellino from the *Pittsburgh Post-Gazette*, we drove quickly across the Bay Bridge to San Francisco's Fisherman's Wharf, where we started to interview people on the scene near Pier 39, where Dan White owned a baked potato stand and had been spotted shortly after the shooting.

It was scary, eerie, and exciting, all at the same time. We gathered as much information as we could, even speaking with a Fisherman's Wharf Santa Claus, and I called my office. While I knew I was in for an extremely long day with a big football game to cover that night, I eagerly volunteered to write as much as my paper needed on this huge story. So did McHugh, our amazingly talented city columnist, who just happened to be on the trip that week.

Well, suffice to say, our same level of excitement was not detected on the phone with my office.

"You can write something if you want to," the editor in charge said, "but I can't guarantee you it's going to get in the paper."

Excuse me. Let me get this straight. I'm taking on all this added pressure and work to give *Press* readers local bylines on the biggest story on the planet today and you're saying what?

To this day, it is still hard to fathom.

Well, I didn't write anything, as much as I wanted to. I covered the Steelers-49ers game that night and made just a single reference to the shooting in my stories.

When I got home the next day, there were four wire stories and several photos in the *Pittsburgh Press* of the shooting.

Nobody ever said anything to me about the issue. Nobody ever apologized for trying to extinguish a 27-year-old reporter's journalistic fire.

Fortunately, it was just temporary.

CHAPTER 27

SHELBY STROTHER

I F YOU DIDN'T KNOW SHELBY STROTHER OR WERE UNABLE TO ever read his work, you missed a very unique experience.

And I'm certain that those of you who knew Shelby and have missed him dearly since his death, at only 44, from liver cancer in 1991, have never met anyone else quite like him.

Shelby worked for several different newspapers—*Orlando Sentinel, Cocoa Today, Melbourne Times, St. Pete Times, Denver Post,* and *Detroit News*—but he wrote to please himself, brandishing a special sensitivity and humor with a flair seldom seen, and certainly not in publications you could once buy for a quarter.

Surely, no editor on this earth could have entered a morning news meeting with any of the story ideas that formed in Shelby's wild brain, let alone mold them into a tearjerker on deadline.

Shelby interviewed fortune tellers at Super Bowls when nobody else thought to do so. He interviewed people at a leper colony for a column. He once found a dwarf bar, complete with little tables and shortened pinball machines. He found a bar in Miami

Beach, with his buddy Tom Archdeacon, where a guy called "The Man Who Stares at the Dirt" would hang out every day, so named because one day he was staring down near the sidewalk and spotted a $100 bill.

Shelby's written words carried the same smile he did—a soft, sheepish grin that signaled you were about to read something that came from his soul, not a typewriter, with a chuckle tucked into every paragraph.

Florida-born in Coral Gables and usually wearing a flowered Hawaiian shirt, Shelby even converted his readers in Northern cities such as Detroit, where he covered the Pistons and became a great friend of coach Chuck Daly. So close was their relationship that when Shelby died, the Pistons wore black shoulder straps on their jerseys for the rest of the season. I don't know of another writer who was so honored.

The first three rows of the funeral audience all wore their flowered shirts for Shelby. I packed one also when I flew to Detroit having heard of Shelby's worsening condition, but I hoped I wouldn't have to use it.

Racing my rental car from the Detroit airport through icy streets, I got to the hospital about 20 minutes after Shelby passed away, but I was allowed in his room to read a poem I had written for him on the plane from Atlanta. I don't know whether I imagined it and I know it sounds contrived, but I had this weird feeling that Shelby had left his body and was looking down at me from the ceiling as I choked through the words, my tears barely allowing me to focus.

I also never imagined that Shelby's skin would feel so warm when I grabbed his hand, hardly what you would expect nearly a half hour after death. The nurses told me they were more than a little freaked out about it and were waiting to move him, not quite sure what to do.

I always felt this was Shelby's way of showing us that not even death could take the warmth from him, at least not right away, anyway.

I first met Shelby in the summer of 1973, when I took a job with the Brevard County edition of the *Orlando Sentinel-Star*, in Cocoa, Fla. Walking into the small bureau office in coat and tie—not particularly comfortable for June in Florida—and carrying a briefcase, I passed a guy with a walrus mustache, flowered shirt, and well-worn white bucks, and took a seat in my office.

A few moments later, I saw the first Shelby grin of thousands and the man said softly, "You tryin' to make me look bad?"

He was chuckling when he said it, and so was I.

We hit it off immediately.

Although I would end up staying in the job for only a few months—let's just call it a journalistic miscalculation—the fact that the experience brought me to Shelby made it genuinely worthwhile.

We hung out at a local bar that attracted space program people called the "Missile Lounge."

We drank beer on the beach, talked about writers we loved to read, and occasionally saw astronauts at the grocery store.

We knew the Cocoa Bureau of the *Orlando Sentinel-Star* was only a temporary address for our careers and that many better places and publications were ahead of us.

We ended up following each other to NFL games, Super Bowls, and college bowl games for more than 20 years. We were fans of each other's writing and, most of all, of each other.

I sometimes think about Shelby's hilarious quirks. Like those amazing cricket sounds he could do in, say, an elevator, making everyone's eyes search toward the corners. Or if we were sitting at a bar and Shelby just happened to realize he had sipped a few beers too many, he might glance over at me, raise his eyebrows, grin that Shelby grin and announce, "I'm blown away!"

We all have been, too, since you left us, my friend. I look forward to continuing where we left off.

CHAPTER 28

TEENER BASEBALL

I'M ONLY INCLUDING THIS INSTALLMENT BECAUSE MANY DECADES later, it's an episode in my sporting life that still cracks me up. It has nothing to do with newspapers or the golf business, but I think you will enjoy it.

I was 13 and playing in my hometown of Palmyra's VFW Teener Baseball League when our coach, for family reasons, had to leave the team.

We were 8-2 at the time and playing pretty good baseball, with me at either third base or pitching. However, if we didn't find a new coach very soon, we were going to be disbanded and forced to forfeit all our games.

But then Don Hershey came to the rescue.

Well, sort of, anyway.

The good news was that Don was happy to help our cause. The bad news was that he knew virtually nothing about baseball as the owner of Hershey's Funeral Home beyond the awareness that the team with the most runs usually wins.

He couldn't hit infield practice without trying to kill us, often firing another grounder at you while you had just crouched down to field his first one.

This is why we called him "Slugger."

He was a decent enough guy; just clueless about what to do as a coach.

He had us bunt with two strikes.

If you came around third and rounded the base, trying to draw a throw, Don might grab you by the arm to stop you, which, of course, is not allowed.

If he pinch-hit for you, he thought he could put you back in the field in the next inning.

But at least we had a coach, and we were still playing baseball.

Because we had a funeral director for a coach, though, it made for some strange situations.

We would all meet at the funeral home to depart for the games as a group, but if it looked like a rainstorm might be forming, Don was known to declare that we might as well not go. We had to explain to him that while it was indeed possible that the game might be canceled, we still had to show up at the field and at least wait it out for a while.

Did I happen to mention that we went to the games in both his funeral limo and the hearse?

Or that because of his laughable hitting talents, one of our players, Jim Lewis, once put a sign on the hearse that said, "Slugger's Body Shop?"

The hearse was kind of creepy and, of course, smelled like flowers back there—a bit unsettling as we stretched out in the back of the vehicle in our baseball uniforms.

The highlight of every trip was coming to a stoplight, pulling up next to a car, and suddenly throwing open the curtains of the hearse.

We could hardly stop laughing at the horrified expressions from those who never would have suspected that a baseball team might be positioned where a coffin should have been.

The season, on the other hand, could have used a funeral march. We finished 10-8, losing six of eight games after Don took over.

Thank goodness, he went back to his day job.

CHAPTER 29

BOB COUSY

WHEN I WAS A JUNIOR AND SENIOR IN HIGH SCHOOL, I HAD a sweet summer job that didn't produce much in the way of income but was outstanding just the same. I worked in the Pro Shop at Hershey Country Club, cleaning clubs, selling golf balls or shirts—and even candy bars—making just $55 a week (a $5 raise the next year for $60). The perks were very nice, however, for an 18-year-old kid. I got to eat big bacon cheeseburgers and steak fries off the menu for lunch, play a lot of golf, and dress like a golf pro, even if I wasn't able to play like one.

A decent amount of celebrities came through HCC in those days to mostly play the West Course, which hosted the 1940 PGA Championship (won by Byron Nelson) and even had Ben Hogan as its head pro from 1941-51.

In the late '60s and early '70s, one of the most notable big names to pass through was Bob Cousy, the ex-Boston Celtic legend.

Cousy would come to Hershey CC every summer as the guest of another New Englander, our member Freddie Smith (whom he called

"Fleddy" in his New York/Boston-ese), and walk 36 holes every day on those thick, strong legs that powered him for so many years on the basketball court.

Whenever Cousy called and I answered, "Pro Shop, Glenn speaking," he would say, "Glenn, it's Bob Cousy."

Then I would say, "Cooz, who you got today."

How cool was that for an 18-year-old kid? Needless to say, I got quite a kick out of it.

One morning Cousy was out playing his usual round with Freddie when my head pro, Jay Weitzel, came into the pro shop and asked, "Where's Cooz?"

"On about No. 6, I would guess, with Freddie," I said.

Whereupon, Jay replied, "Jesus Christ, Glennie, he's supposed to play with the Governor (Pennsylvania Gov. Ray Shafer) today!"

Then Jay said, "Jesus Christ, Glennie, go out there and tell him!"

OK, Jay, whatever you say. You're the boss.

So, I hopped in a cart and drove out five minutes or so to the par-5 6th hole just as Cousy and Freddie were walking off the tee box.

I pulled up across from them in the fairway and waved a finger for Cousy to wander over to my cart.

"What's up, Glenn?" he said, leaving his caddie and approaching me.

"Did you know you were supposed to play with the Governor today?" I said to the greatest ballhandler in NBA history.

Cousy digested the information, paused for a few seconds, and said, calmly, "Tell the Governor to go fuck himself."

As you might expect, I became an even bigger Bob Cousy fan that day.

CHAPTER 30

TIGER WOODS

I HAVE TO BE HONEST; I WAS GLAD TO BE NO LONGER COVERING golf or working for a newspaper when the Tiger Woods controversy exploded in 2009.

Why would I say that? Well, because I assure you, my relationship with Tiger would have prompted my editors, with absolutely no concern about my future dealings with the game's greatest player, to find out immediately why he rammed his Escalade into a tree near his home in Windermere, Fla., sending his career into oblivion.

Or, as David Feherty so aptly described it years later when Tiger started dating Olympic ski champion Lindsey Vonn, "He met someone who can go downhill faster than he did."

If you were covering golf then, this was a story to investigate carefully, especially considering the amount of misinformation circulating. The golf writers who regularly covered Tiger Woods couldn't make him a daily punch line as the late-night talk show hosts were doing. Legitimate journalists would have to cover Tiger later after all of the chaos ended, and if you don't think Tiger and his representatives kept track of who treated him fairly and who didn't, then you didn't know the man or his people.

Golf writers like my friends Doug Ferguson of the *Associated Press* or Bob Harig, then of *ESPN.com*, managed it, but you can bet there were occasions when they had to try and reason with overzealous editors. Heck, I had to do it many times over the years with just routine Tiger stories.

As I said, I felt relieved to have been watching this one from the sidelines.

I'm happy to say my memories of Tiger and our professional relationship were mostly about golf, with a few exceptions, most notably the Martha Burk mess with Augusta National in 2003 regarding women members. I spent many years cultivating that relationship and I'm proud to say Tiger trusted me as a reporter and friend.

I covered the 10 majors he won from 1997 to 2005, beginning with that first Masters. Hard as it is to believe now, he was winning so much back then, we were bored with writing the same story week after week and prayed for something different. Considering his staggering pace, nobody could have imagined Tiger going 11 years between major wins (2008 U.S. Open to the 2019 Masters).

I often walked the course during his rounds, or for at least the front nine, and he always appreciated seeing me out there. And that often helped me down the road when I might have been critical about a certain on-course decision. Because I was out there observing, I had more credibility and room to criticize.

And most tour players are like that. Even the frequently grumpy Vijay Singh. If they see you out there, they treat you differently. The guy they hate most is the one who camps in the press center all day, uses the interview transcripts as gospel with no knowledge or concern about their context, and takes potshots.

For the most part, I had tremendous access to Tiger. I hardly ever went through his main PR guy, Mark Steinberg, but instead just set it up with Tiger personally. I would say, for example, OK, Tiger, how about Tuesday of the Match Play Championship at La Costa after your practice round? Good for me, he would probably say.

And that would be it. Usually, it would be one-on-one, unless somebody wandered by and saw us in the locker room or wherever, and then a crowd would form. (Usually, that was Doug Ferguson, who had a sixth sense about Tiger being interviewed somewhere without him in attendance. Fergie is the best, and there is nobody even close. If we were trying to sneak out for golf on a Monday or Tuesday, I often asked him to join us. That way, I could at least keep my eye on him and limit his exposure to the players. But it usually didn't work. He still beat everyone most of the time.)

For those of us who would travel to cover maybe 15-18 PGA Tour events a year, Tiger was great. It's the stranger in the big press room who would make us all look bad by flipping around Tiger's words and trying to catch him in something controversial. Usually that type of "reporter" wasn't even a golf writer, but some celebrity page hack.

Make no mistake, Tiger occasionally could be very profane and I'm sure still is. But, to me, that's what made him normal. Plus, it was hilarious. We couldn't play like him, obviously, but we could curse pretty darned well. (If you ever heard one of my outbursts while reading in disbelief a story that had just been ruined by an editor, you'd know what I mean.)

Many tour players were known to release an F-bomb when they were out of microphone range. It was no big deal, even though the fans were plenty shocked when it happened. Usually, they're self-deprecating eruptions, especially the ones from Tiger. Playing at Colonial in 1997 at age 20 after consecutive wins at Augusta and the Byron Nelson, Tiger flew a green with his wedge and stunned the Fort Worth crowd with a solid, "FUCK ME!"

Covering Tiger back then was very exciting. More than not, anything you wrote about Tiger was front-page material and my paper, the *Atlanta Journal-Constitution*, sent me everywhere to follow him.

I remember one year during the Match Play trying to get a few words with him coming off the range at LaCosta for a pre-Masters story I was doing. He was short on time and heading back to his room, clear across the resort, and said, "Walk with me."

With my tape recorder going and trying to scribble notes on the run, which is not easy, we went through a couple of lobbies, the kitchen, a couple of hallways, past the tennis courts and the spa, before eventually going through a door, up some steps and coming out on the other side of the development, at least a 10-minute walk from where we started. I had no idea where we were.

When we reached his room, Tiger said, "You good?"

"Yes, thanks, see you later," I said.

When I turned around, I noticed the PGA Tour's chief security guy had been right behind us the whole time, through every passageway and stairway, keeping golf's star attraction in his sights.

I smiled at him. He waved and headed back to tournament headquarters.

They were very different times, to be sure.

At the 2001 PGA at the Atlanta Athletic Club, I waited for Tiger when he came off the 9th hole after a Tuesday practice round. We were walking through a roped-off area of frenzied fans, mostly kids, sticking pieces of paper, photos, and magazines toward him to sign. The ropes on either side of us were probably a little too close and suddenly Tiger winced as the corner of a book was pushed into his eye. He yelled, held his hand over his eye, and fled to the locker room. I followed him, concerned that he was really hurt and that his tournament status might be in jeopardy.

At his locker, he said, rubbing his eye, "I'm fine. Happens all the time."

The particularly refreshing part about Tiger's comeback, which culminated in his 2019 Masters win, was the personality he started showing to the fans. The golf writers would see Tiger's lighter side all the time in sessions with just a few of us, but in his eyes-to-the-ground days of the late 1990s and early 2000s, you would never see him high-fiving kids or grinning so easily to the galleries.

Maybe it's because he has kids now. Maybe it's because after being so physically and emotionally wrecked, he appreciates everything so much more now. Maybe it's because in his farewell tour, if that's what this is, there's no pressure any longer to be what his late father demanded of him. He ruined a marriage, which resulted in an expensive divorce, and almost ruined an iconic career. Everything from 2018 on was gravy and Tiger seems like a guy who now never takes any day for granted.

When I think about those early days, two events always come to mind for me. Neither of them is widely discussed or recognized for their meaningfulness, but they were both very big deals.

How many people even remember that when at Stanford in November of 1994, the 18-year-old Woods was robbed at knifepoint behind his dormitory and could have been killed? According to the police report, Tiger had just returned from New York, where he had received an award, when a guy yelled his name, held a knife to his throat, stole his gold chain necklace and a watch, then used the butt end of the knife to strike him in the jaw. Tiger was knocked to the pavement but escaped serious injury.

Just like that, the young phenom could have been vanquished.

Gone, never to completely change the game of golf and dominate for a dozen years.

I asked Tiger about the incident a couple of times, and he never wanted to talk about it. Clearly, it says a lot that both Tiger and his father were able to put the matter behind them so easily, but it always made me think about how fragile life is and how the world was nearly robbed of this mind-boggling, once-in-a-lifetime performance.

The second event came at the 1997 Masters, which all golf followers know as Tiger's first victory at Augusta, by 12 shots, which changed the sport almost overnight as this multi-cultural kid from California grabbed the world's attention.

When the tournament ended that day, we were on the Augusta National grounds interviewing workers who gushed about the significance of an African-American player winning at a place not known for its diversity.

A couple of hours earlier, as he finished his round, Fuzzy Zoeller was being interviewed by CNN underneath the famous big oak tree in front of the clubhouse. Asked about Woods' almost certain victory as his huge lead grew on the back nine, Fuzzy uttered those famous comments, eventually setting off a global outrage.

"The little boy's driving it well and he's putting well," Zoeller said. "He's doing everything it takes to win. So, you know what you guys do when he gets in here? Pat him on the back, say congratulations, enjoy it, and tell him not to serve fried chicken next year...... or collard greens."

A stupid redneck comment? Yes. Racially insensitive? Probably. But to be honest, just typical Fuzzy.

Fortunately, as it turns out, CNN's Jim Huber, a good friend of mine, was the real hero that day.

He saved a stupid comment from dominating an enormous event.

I'm not sure why Jim chose not to give Fuzzy's comments to the network for immediate broadcast, but for the golf world's sake, I'm very glad for his decision.

Probably he was just protecting Fuzzy because he knew he had a cocktail or two and was prone to say redneck-type things. Maybe he didn't want Tiger's historical day spoiled, either. But the fact is, if Fuzzy's comments had gone on the air before Tiger finished his round—or anytime that same day—it would have overshadowed a socially mammoth 12-shot win and the beginning of an incredible era at Augusta. Fried chicken and collard greens would have dominated our stories, not record-setting golf, and that truly would have been a shame.

As it turns out, the Zoeller video was not released until six days later, when a CNN editor happened to be going through Huber's tapes and noticed it. Late or not, it still caused a huge ruckus, as you surely recall, but thank God it didn't taint one of the greatest days in golf history.

Jim is gone now, and I can't ask him exactly what he was thinking, but I've always been happy for the judgment he made, and Tiger should be, too.

In the fall of 1997 the International Management Group (IMG), which represented Tiger, invited 12 writers down to Bay Hill to spend the day with him. I was flattered to have been included and I happily accepted.

It was incredible access for the time, when Tigermania had been building hugely since his win at Augusta in April, followed by a victory the next week at the Byron Nelson, and then later at the Western Open.

We all sat around a big table at Bay Hill and discussed any number of subjects through breakfast and lunch, then went outside, ostensibly, to each play three holes with Tiger. The trouble was, it rained and only a few guys got to play. The rest of us merely hit balls with him on the range, which was nerve-wracking enough. His 4-iron was traveling farther than our drives.

It was a great experience, though, to build an early relationship with Tiger and it certainly helped me over the next decade, when he positioned me with a dozen or so other writers whom he trusted and could speak freely off the record without fear of getting burned. Which was important. Back then there were scads of media people—not golf writers typically—trying to burn him, twist his words around or, well, just rip him because racism still lives, unfortunately.

From merely the standpoint of golf talent, Tiger stood alone.

I remember being on the practice range at LaCosta during the Match Play Championship, late in the day, watching Tiger hit 3-wood after 3-wood, with that perfect little draw he used to play, up against the mountains in the background. It was machine-like, to be sure, and I had never seen anything quite like it before.

Pete McDaniel of *Golf Digest* and I were following him at Bay Hill one day on a leisurely Friday afternoon when, while walking off the tee box, he was laughing with his playing partners. Turns out, he had killed a fly on the face of his driver and was showing it to them. I don't know how often that happens, but it seemed rather unusual to me.

When Tiger played in the Tour Championship at East Lake, which used to be scheduled during Halloween Week, he often pulled out a gag Afro wig and walked up the 18th fairway with it on, saying "Boo!" to kids sitting along the grass, and then howling.

It always cracked me up and when he didn't wear it one year, I asked him about it.

"I don't know where it is," he said. "I think I left it in the back of a cab somewhere."

I was at the 1998 clinic that Tiger conducted for Atlanta city kids at Browns Mill Golf Course, south of downtown, and because of the extreme attention he was drawing then, a security force of six or eight guys with earphones was common, typically forming a moving bubble around him. The rumor was that automatic weapons were stowed inside Tiger's golf bag in case of trouble. Everything went smoothly, however, and every kid who left the event that day had a new hero.

Two years before, when Tiger turned pro and exploded onto the PGA Tour scene, an appearance in Georgia had generated a much different kind of publicity. Having received a sponsor exemption to play in the Buick Challenge at Callaway Gardens in Pine Mountain, Ga., where he was also to receive the Fred Haskins Award as the nation's outstanding collegiate player, Tiger held a press conference and played a 9-hole practice round on Tuesday.

That night, however, Tiger decided he was exhausted and told his then-agent, Hughes Norton, that he wished to withdraw. Which he did, drawing an immense amount of negative, but warranted publicity. (I've always felt that Tiger's agent should have suggested he remain long enough to receive the Haskins Award, and then withdraw. Tiger came back to Callaway Gardens in November of that year to receive the award and apologized to the Haskins committee, but the damage had been done.)

When Tiger suffered his horrific SUV accident in Southern California on Feb 23, 2021, I had a sick feeling in my stomach all day and didn't lose it until the next morning when, despite the gory details of his leg injuries, I knew he had survived. My first thoughts were that while Tiger's competitive career might be over, I only hoped he eventually would be able to at least play fun golf with his kids. Anybody who saw Tiger and young Charlie gleefully compete in the 2020 Father-Son tournament could tell how special these upcoming years were going to be for them.

I also thought that day about the irony of his young PGA Tour friends like Rory McIlroy or Justin Thomas always kidding him about his skinny legs, and it's something that I always noticed, along with his relatively thin wrists. Despite an expanded upper body that was developed through strength training, everything about Tiger's lower body from the waist down was still small-boned and normal for such a great athlete. I've always felt this contributed to his long-time back and knee issues.

And, sadly, it's quite possible that those physical facts made his right leg or ankle more likely to shatter under the stress of a severe accident than, say, a thick-legged guy like Jon Rahm.

But at least Tiger survived and was alone in the vehicle. Had he been driving a cramped sports car at home—his Porsche perhaps—rather than a brand-new Genesis SUV with all the finest safety features, he clearly might not have made it.

As much as Tiger wants to be reunited with his Pop, I thanked God it wasn't at this moment.

There is no way to determine the length or success rate of his on-going recovery. I am concerned about his pain, which has been vast, and a previous issue with painkillers following surgeries far less complex than those from his accident.

It bothered me when in the early days after the accident, Tiger's detractors were out there in force, making unfair judgments about the accident and his past.

The racism that still exists toward Tiger has always shocked and troubled me, and it's even more disturbing that it would continue after such a tragedy.

Needless to say, I'm delighted that Tiger miraculously returned, starting with the Father-Son tournament in 2021, which I saw in person for a day at the Ritz-Carlton Golf Club in Orlando. My daughter,

Jessica, was then working at the Ritz in sales and came up with some tickets at the last minute.

Though Tiger was walking painfully, with my grandsons Tyler and Bryan, we had a blast watching him and Charlie.

That Tiger would go on to make the cut at the 2022 Masters and PGA, only to fall short at the 150th Open at St. Andrews, it was great to see him playing competitively again, his walking agony notwithstanding.

I'm thrilled that he is enjoying himself more than ever, feeding off crowd energy and love. His fans seemingly have closed the door on his scandal of more than a decade ago. Sadly, his detractors never will.

While it's a shame Tiger didn't feel comfortable connecting with galleries this way when performing in his peak years, that's the way his father taught him, to shut everything out and keep focused.

I'm also glad Earl Woods was around long enough to enjoy some Father-Son rewards, too. I remember him playing one year as Tiger's partner in the Pebble Beach National Pro-Am and I was at Poppy Hills when they teed off for the first round.

After Tiger drove nicely, Earl was up next, hitting from his tee a bit further up. Perhaps not sufficiently warmed up, Earl topped a drive that hardly got to the fairway.

Barely out of his downswing, Earl quipped, looking back at his famous son and then to the gallery, "Yeah, but you should see my horse!"

CHAPTER 31

JACK NICKLAUS

G ETTING TO KNOW JACK NICKLAUS WHILE COVERING GOLF WAS one of my biggest thrills, as it was for any of us who enjoyed a first-name relationship with perhaps the game's greatest player.

When I started doing research for this book, I was astounded to realize how many stories during my 20 years of covering golf involved Jack Nicklaus. Whether it happened to be a major championship, a special achievement, or a personal experience, Nicklaus was the main character more than he was not.

For a kid who grew up in Arnold Palmer country, that was saying something.

My early connection with Nicklaus came during my college years when working in the Pro Shop at Hershey Country Club on term breaks. My boss, Jay Weitzel, the head pro, had come to Hershey as an assistant from Scioto Country Club in Columbus, Ohio, where Jack grew up as famed instructor Jack Grout's star pupil. Hardly a day went by back then, Jay said, that he didn't watch "Jackie" hitting balls on the range with Grout. That Nicklaus became the game's dominant player certainly was no surprise to Jay.

Little did I know how prominent Jack Nicklaus would become in my golf life. That I would often walk with his wonderful wife, Barbara, at Augusta, watching Jack play in the Masters until his last one in 2005. That we would all walk together at Doral's Gold Course one day, rooting for their son, Gary, to secure his PGA Tour card.

Or that we would exchange letters and flowers, when I was recovering from kidney cancer surgery in 1998, and then the following year, when Jack underwent hip replacement surgery.

I remember just before the surgery asking Jack about the type of material that was going to be used for his new hip.

"Titanium?" I asked.

"No," he said. "Ceramic."

"Really?" I said. "I always figured you as a persimmon guy."

He laughed, but not as loudly as that day in the Masters media center, during one of his marathon press conferences, often on Wednesday afternoon on the eve of the tournament. Jack was going on and on, no doubt arguing for dialing back the golf ball, when *Atlanta Journal* sports editor Furman Bisher stood up at his chair and slid out toward the aisle, causing chairs to clatter and drawing Nicklaus' attention.

"Furman," Jack asked, "aren't you going to wait for my answer to the question?"

Said Furman, without hesitation as he kept moving toward the exit, "Jack, when you get to be as old as I am, you learn to trust your kidneys!"

The 1986 Masters, of course, was when the whole world became a Nicklaus fan.

I often think about how fortunate we all were to witness what happened at that Masters, probably the best one ever, when Jack won his sixth green jacket at age 46, 11 years after his fifth one. I wasn't out there covering golf in the '60s and '70s when Jack was in his prime, but here he was in 1986, giving all of us an encore with a final-round 65 and a performance that even now seems hard to fathom. I'm sure that's how the writers (and some of the players) felt in 2019, when Tiger Woods' comeback brought him a fifth green jacket, realizing how it must have been in the mid-'90s and early 2000s for us to experience, when Woods was dominating the game.

I wasn't the lead golf writer for the *AJC* in 1986. I was Tom McCollister's backup guy when I wasn't occupied with NFL responsibilities during my "off-season." Hard-core golf fans probably know the story about Tom writing in advance of the tournament that Nicklaus, at the time playing poorly, was too old to win another Masters at 46 and might consider hanging it up as a serious Augusta contender.

Of course, Nicklaus' friend, John Montgomery, pasted the *AJC* clipping on the fridge at the home they were renting that week. Every time Jack read it, it irked him even more, not in an angry way, but as an incentive to get his Augusta act together.

To say the least, he did, and when Jack came into the media center after his amazing victory, he sat down and said, grinning, "Where's Tom McCollister?"

It was said playfully, more in an I-guess-I showed-you sort of way. As Jack was informed, Tom was still writing on deadline in the adjacent media work area and not yet present in the interview room.

When Tom finally entered the room, Jack looked up, smiled, and said, "Thanks, Tom!"

Said McCollister, grinning as he found his seat, "Anything I can do to help."

Tom's next line was the best one, but not too many people—probably not even Jack—heard it, still laughing at the previous exchange.

"Watson wants me to write about him next year," Tom said, bringing a roar from his colleagues around him.

When Jack teed off at the 18th that day, I decided that I wasn't about to watch this historic finish on one of the media center TVs, which were a pleasant alternative when stuck in your seat close to deadline. Because I was only doing post-tournament stories, I was free to roam until then, so I sprinted out to the 18th hole, grabbing a spot about 10 rows deep at the back of the green, just in time to see Jack tap in for par and hug son Jackie, his caddie.

I wrote the lead story and a sidebar for the *Journal*, our afternoon paper, that night, setting up at the dining room table of our rented house. That was the beauty of writing for the afternoon paper. You had time to sit back, take a few deep breaths, and digest what you had witnessed, and if ever there was a time for deep breathing, this was it. Here are the first few paragraphs from my lead story:

```
AUGUSTA—They not only said it couldn't be done.
They said it couldn't be pondered.
    Sure, Jack Nicklaus was going to win a sixth
Masters at age 46 with his golf game in shambles.
Right. And Phil Niekro's going to win 30 and next
week they're going to open up Augusta National to
the public.
    Tell me some more miracles.
    OK, are you ready?
    Jack Nicklaus won his sixth Masters Sunday at
age 46.
```

That was No. 1 for Nicklaus stories, but for me, a close second was his final Open Championship in 2005 at St. Andrews. I walked every shot with him that day and every step was special. He even tapped me on the butt with the grip of his club walking off the 11th tee, appreciating my presence.

As he rocketed a tee shot at the 18th hole into a cloudless Scotland sky, we were leaning on the Road Hole wall behind the tee box. When we stood up to follow his drive, a Scottish woman behind us pleaded in a deep brogue, "Please sit down! It's OUR moment, too!"

During Jack's late competitive years, there surely were some lean times. I recall him on the range at Bay Hill one day, hitting snap hooks with regularity, which was almost unfathomable considering the fade game he made famous. The late Phil Ritson, the famed Australian instructor, was standing next to me, shaking his head in disbelief.

In a self-deprecating mood, Jack said to me one day at the Atlanta Athletic Club, where he was visiting for a course design consultation, "Everybody's always wanted to play like Nicklaus. Now they can."

It's funny. As much as everyone talks about Jack's 1986 Masters win at age 46, when he opened with a 74 and closed with a 65, I think it was equally incredible that in 1998 at age 58 he tied for sixth. He was two shots off the lead nearly halfway through the final round, with four birdies in his first seven holes.

David Duval, who tied for second behind Mark O'Meara, told *USA Today* that day, "He's Jack Nicklaus. Of course, I thought he could win."

Jack didn't make such a threat in 2000 when he played his final U.S. Open at Pebble Beach, but I was with a cluster of other writers behind the 18th green on Friday afternoon, watching his towering second shot arrive at the front of the putting surface. Never before had there been such a fuss for a guy shooting a second-round 82 and missing the cut by eight shots. That Jack three-putted for par didn't really make any difference. At 60, the Golden Bear was still hitting par-5s in two in a major.

After Tom McCollister's famous story in 1986, I always used to tell Jack, "I don't care how you're playing coming into the Masters, we're never writing you off again."

Good thing, too. Imagine if Jack had made a few more birdies in 1998.

CHAPTER 32

AUGUSTA AND THE MASTERS

THE MASTERS WILL ALWAYS BE SPECIAL TO ME. FROM FLIPPING through the pages of *Sport* magazine as a kid, imagining what it would be like to see this incredible scenery in person, to being fortunate to cover 20 Masters and enjoy this unique inside look at the most revered of golf's majors.

Not to mention being able to play the course in 1999.

While every writer who has reported on the Masters wishes that Augusta National's politics had not taken so long to make a progressive turn, there was no better place in the entire world to be that week, especially if you loved golf as much as I did.

I'd also like to think that the *Atlanta Journal-Constitution* had the best group of writers in the country covering during Masters week. How about a columnist lineup of Furman Bisher, Dave Kindred, Steve Hummer, and Mark Bradley, all sitting together on press row? And Tom Stinson, Jack Wilkinson, and Michelle Hiskey doing features? Pretty impressive. I was lucky to have been working with them.

Ben Crenshaw won my first year there (1984). I didn't know him very well then, but later, especially after his 1995 victory, we became good friends, always met up during Masters week at some point, and exchanged letters over the years. Not that long ago, I gave him a copy of a radio interview conducted with Bobby Jones in the 1960s. He was tremendously grateful and penned a thank-you letter to me that remains one of my favorite mementos.

I always looked forward to shaking hands with Ben, too, hoping that weathered mitt would transfer some putting magic over to me.

Whenever I tell people outside of my sportswriter fraternity that I was fortunate to cover the Masters for so many years, they are always jealous and can't imagine how much fun it must have been. As I mentioned before, it was wonderful indeed to look out every day at the most beautiful spot in golf, however, there was still plenty of hard work. It wasn't all azalea watching, pimento cheese sandwiches, and lunch on the clubhouse lawn.

With my paper, the *AJC*, and the *Augusta Chronicle* being the unofficial papers of record, there was intense scrutiny during Masters Week—from readers, your fellow sportswriters, and your editors. When it's the biggest story in golf and a relative home game for you, being only 120 miles from Augusta, everything you write is read by your peers every day.

It's flattering and frightening, exciting and excruciating, all at the same time. If you write something you're genuinely pleased with, you hope everyone sees it and talks about it all day. But mess something up and you want to load up every Media Center copy of the *AJC* into the back of a truck and find the nearest landfill.

In my early years, I was a small part of the Masters team, maybe one of six people. At that time, the NFL was my main beat, with golf my secondary one, behind Tom McCollister, our veteran beat man and one of my closest friends. Because I wasn't running the show, which meant organizing the story assignments and writing the lead story every day, I could take a sidebar idea from Tom, spend hours on the course gathering details, and then casually wander into the Media Center at mid-afternoon to start writing. It was a blast.

That's completely different from being the leader of the team. If you're deciding, along with the editor on site, which stories are to be written and by whom, you spend most of the day in the Media Center, close to the TVs, from where you can see everything that's going on and adjust the coverage, if necessary.

It was pressure-packed, but tremendously satisfying when that last story was filed every night. Believe me, that first sip of your first beer in the green Masters cup was an unmatched journalistic pleasure.

I was very lucky to have worked with those people I already mentioned at the Masters every year, including the legendary Furman Bisher, but I was closest to the two Tom's—Tom McCollister and Tom Stinson.

TMac was my beloved mentor, friend, and frequent golf partner. Being a dozen or so years older than most of the younger writers, TMac was a sort of father figure to us and taught me so much about the daily business of being a golf writer. Most importantly, the trust factor. Golf relationships often took years to cultivate, and people trusted that Tom would write about them fairly and accurately.

When TMac died in 1999 of a car accident at only 61, it was one of the darkest days of my life. I still miss him and think about him fondly every April at Masters time. I was in Miami covering the Doral-Ryder Open when I got the horrible call from my office. Numb from the news, Steve Hershey and I sat in the Doral bar that night, reminiscing about Tom over several beers, and we both agreed that nobody in the business was more respected and loved. Ironically, when the accident happened, TMac was about to return to golf, this time as my partner, a couple of days later. It was all so very sad.

As the golf writer for the *Journal-Constitution*, the relationship with Augusta National was always a delicate one. Not as delicate, however, as it was for the *Augusta Chronicle*, whose owner, Billy Morris, was an Augusta National member and even assisted with official player interviews during Masters week.

In 2003 I had written a Sunday story during the Martha Burk controversy about Augusta National's aging membership. One of our best artists, Vernon Carne, had included a graphic that depicted the more senior Augusta members stumbling around the grounds in green jackets and mummy bandages. Very funny, unless you happened to own a green jacket, that is, and were well past the AARP qualifying age.

Someone had alerted Martha Gay, who always checked in the media up front, about the story, and when I approached, she said in that syrupy drawl, "GLEE-in, would you happen to have a copy of today's PAY-puh?"

I did indeed, and it was stuck under my arm, but as much as I loved Martha, I wasn't going to help with her investigation.

So, I said, "No, I don't, but I'll try to find one for you."

Of course, I never did, but I'm sure someone else produced one before the lunchtime pimento cheese sandwiches were brought out.

The only one of the Masters big shots I ever knew very well was Billy Payne, and that was during the time he ran the press center, well before he became chairman.

This was post-Atlanta Olympics time, of course, and I was one of the few *AJC* reporters with whom he spoke. Anyone who covered the Olympics back when he chaired the Games, had by then thoroughly pissed him off and he usually didn't take their calls.

On the other hand, I represented Billy's true love, golf, and he enjoyed talking with me—even when it concerned the women's membership controversy—and while not allowing himself to be quoted, at least he listened and trusted me.

Maybe he wasn't aware of my past Masters transgressions. Indeed, many years before I had been thoroughly chastised for the "crime" of quoting the Augusta National agronomist about the pre-tournament condition of the azaleas.

True story.

As strange as that sounds, it was always a big deal as to whether the flowers would be brilliant for the tournament. Maybe they were well past their peak and completely gone, or perhaps they were slow to open from a cool spring and disappointingly muted.

Nobody back then but the Chairman was allowed to be quoted—anywhere. It's not much different today, though quite a bit looser from Billy Payne's regime on and continues with the personable Fred Ridley in charge.

There were always stories about how the greenskeeping crew supposedly iced down the azaleas if the weeks approaching were unseasonably warm, ostensibly to slow their opening and preserve them for the tournament.

Or that if the spring was unusually cold, rumors persisted that hair dryers were sometimes used to open up the blooms at the precise time.

They were just legends, and there's nothing to support them.

That said, I always wondered if somewhere on the grounds a pine straw factory might have existed. How else could you explain that fresh stuff out there every day, all day?

Just kidding. Probably.

Starting in the mid-'90s, after the tournament people got to know me, I was allowed to buy a ticket and happily shared it with my wife Nora and some very grateful, often giddy friends.

George Fisher, one of my old neighbors at Eagle Watch Golf Club in Woodstock, told his wife after I had contacted him with the good news, "Honey, tomorrow morning I'm going to heaven."

One year I took my urologist, Howard Rottenberg, who performed my kidney cancer surgery in 1998. Another time, the guest was my chiropractor, Larry Reuter, who got me back playing golf again through years of treatment. One year it was Stanley Parker, a close friend and old neighbor in Dunwoody, Ga., who got the call, and to this day he still talks about the splendor of the experience.

It was a blast getting them on the phone the day before and saying, "How'd you like to go to the Masters tomorrow as my guest?"

I felt like Michael Anthony in that old TV show, "The Millionaire," showing up with a seven-figure, tax-free check to unsuspecting individuals.

Not that Nora didn't appreciate the badge when it was available to her, but her staying power for a whole day of elbowing through the crowds was less than impressive. Shortly after lunch, she might say, "I'm going to go back to the house and watch it on TV."

"You're going to what?" I would say, stunned. "I could get $2,500 for that badge." (Which I wouldn't do, of course, but I'm sure somebody would.)

In my early days of covering the Masters, in the '80s, I would get sidebar assignments that were usually interesting and fun, as I could often spend several hours with a player, covering him all around the course. (The Masters, however, is the only golf tournament in the world, as far as I know, where the media isn't allowed under the gallery ropes. You walk with the patrons and are not afforded the unobstructed view you get at other tournaments, so long as you're holding the proper credential.)

But sometimes you draw hazardous duty. Like in 1985, when Curtis Strange shot a first-round 80.

After the round, he positioned himself to the right of the practice range, all alone with his caddie, searching for something to somehow survive the cut on Friday.

As soon as he saw me approaching, I got the infamous Curtis glare.

Still seething, he gave a lot of short, grumpy answers and was none too thrilled about having to reconstruct any portion of the disastrous round for me and my readers.

As it turned out, Strange would rally impressively with a second-round 65, was even leading at one point on the back nine on Sunday and eventually tied for second, just two shots behind Bernhard Langer.

Many years later, when Curtis was playing sparsely and working mostly as a TV golf analyst, I refreshed his memory regarding the awkward scene.

"How was I?" he said. "I was good, right?"

"Actually, Curtis," I said, "No, you weren't. Not that I could blame you, but you were awful. You gave me 'the glare.'"

Not often does a media member get invited into the Champions Locker Room at Augusta National, unless maybe you're Dan Jenkins or Furman Bisher. A small area upstairs where the champions share tiny lockers, it used to feature saloon-type doors which allowed you to see who happened to be in the room at the time, eating lunch or changing shoes. Later, they put a regular door there, leaving you with only a little board to the left of the doorway, with brass nameplates, to know who was in the room. A guy with white gloves would place the names or remove them, depending on who was coming or going.

I was invited in there once, by Tommy Aaron, and while I was interviewing him at the table, both Tom Watson and Gay Brewer visited the hallowed area.

It was very cool.

Lunchtime was always a big deal during Masters week. There were unlimited amounts of the famous green-wrapper sandwiches or barbecue in the press center, but during the tournament media credentialed men or women were allowed to eat in the Augusta National clubhouse, even though back then the sign on the first-floor door, coming off the 18th hole and the big oak tree, still said "Gentlemen Only.

When you were able to get a table, you were also allowed to eat on the clubhouse lawn at the white patio tables with the green umbrellas. I'd try to dine there at least once during the week when Nora was there, but the regulars were mostly Augusta members, celebrities, or columnists who had nothing to do until later in the day.

Sometimes when Nora was using my extra badge, since she had no clubhouse access, I would order two big cheeseburgers and steak fries to go, allowing us to sit in the bleachers behind the range while we ate.

This always drew lots of comments from the patrons, who were already tired of pimento cheese or egg salad sandwiches, their 1960s prices notwithstanding.

Walk in with a couple of juicy, medium-rare, half-pound cheeseburgers and you're certain to hear more than one person ask, "Where the hell did you get those?"

It was always a kick to know that my little old media badge allowed it and that even if you arrived in Augusta in a private jet, unless you had a clubhouse pass, you couldn't order a cheeseburger from the Grill and eat it while you watched Jack Nicklaus go through his bag on the range.

And that's something very interesting about the Masters experience as a journalist. On one hand, the tournament people prohibited you from viewing under the gallery ropes. You couldn't even bring a tape recorder onto the course without registering it in the Media Center.

But for that one week you could hang out in the clubhouse just like you were a member.

For those of you who think Augusta and the Masters is all charm and Southern Hospitality, with banjo music playing and Jim Nantz narrating, you haven't been to downtown Augusta. Yes, almost everything inside the gates of Augusta National is high-class and Deep South dominant. And, yes, the mansions down Wheeler Road are always impressive. But wandering around many areas of downtown Augusta in the '80s and '90s was like being on shore leave. The town catered to Masters guests for one week a year. The rest of the time, the economic focal points were inhabitants of nearby Fort Gordon or temporary visitors from the Convention Center.

Suffice to say you weren't going to see any players at the seedier downtown joints. Caddies, yes, but the players mostly stayed in rented homes well off Washington Road.

Tom Stinson and I had more laughs every year during Masters Week than should be allowed. Among other things, in our early, single days of covering the tournament we were known to visit a seedy "adult ballet" club in downtown Augusta called Chicago Lil's, whose logo out front was a dead mouse in a martini glass.

Cute, huh?

It was there that the legendary Shelby Strother once tilted his head back toward the dance floor, placed a $5 bill on his nose, and proclaimed, "The first thing you've got to do is let 'em know you're serious."

We all decided that was great local knowledge.

CHAPTER 33

IN OVER-MY-HEAD GOLF

O
NE OF THE PERKS OF BEING A GOLF WRITER IS THAT occasionally you get to play golf with the tour players you cover, and that's unique to any other sports beat in the newspaper. You will not likely ever enjoy the opportunity to compete on the same field with, say, Patrick Mahomes, or stand in the batter's box to face a 100-mph fastball.

Which is probably a good thing.

I'm going to start with my best tour player experience.

It was in 2002, when Stewart Cink, a Georgia Tech guy and Atlanta resident, made his first Ryder Cup team. My paper, the *Atlanta Journal-Constitution*, was doing a big story on him and we decided to meet on the practice range at TPC Sugarloaf in Duluth, Ga., where Stewart resided and frequently played.

Suddenly, Cink pulled up in a cart and asked, "Do you have your clubs with you?"

"Sure, I always do," I said.

"Good," he said. "Let's go play nine."

Cool, I thought. No time to get nervous overnight, which often happened. Just go play. I was comfortable.

So comfortable, amazingly enough, that I ended up sinking a long putt for birdie on the first hole of Sugarloaf's Pines Nine and took to the second tee box—ONE STROKE UP ON THE RYDER CUP PLAYER!!

Is that the reason Stewart decided to hit two drives off the next tee box, suddenly changing it to just practice? Not likely, but the sportswriter could at least fantasize that Cink didn't want to take any chances with a 7-handicapper somehow playing a dream nine holes.

Well, that didn't happen, of course, but I was still 1-under through seven holes, keeping alive this miraculous mastery.

"Can't believe I'm 1-under," I said to Stewart on the par-5 8th tee box.

This turned out to be the wrong thing to mention.

I promptly took a triple-bogey 8 on the hole and then bogeyed the 9th to finish with a 3-over-par 39.

But I couldn't be too disappointed. You're damn right I'd have taken a 39 standing on that first tee. At least Stewart knew I could play a little.

On not every occasion was that particularly evident. I played twice with Atlanta resident Billy Andrade—once at Atlanta Country Club along with my pal John Marshall, a very long hitter back then who played commendably, and later just with Billy at Capital City Country Club Crabapple, where he shot the easiest 66 I had ever witnessed. I was absolutely awful and seriously embarrassed. Thank God, I was playing with Billy, who at least knew I could play considerably better than I had just demonstrated.

I played in a 1997 media event that allowed three holes each with Tom Kite, Chris DiMarco, and Nancy Lopez. The highlights: Tom

Kite, then the upcoming Ryder Cup captain, raked a bunker for me; and I got a takeaway tip, a hug, and a kiss from Nancy, who is one of my favorite people in golf and always will be.

I played once at Atlanta Country Club with the famed instructor, Bob Toski, who after I hit a crisp wedge to a green on the back nine, said, "Nice swing, Glenn."

OK, God, reel me on up. I'm ready.

The funniest tour player I ever played with was definitely England's Laura Davies, who had me laughing the entire round at Eagles Landing CC in Stockbridge, Ga., home of the LPGA Chick-fil-A Charity Championship.

Me: "I can't believe I hit it in the water twice on the same hole."

Laura: "Well, I must say, you made it look easy."

Laura: "I play so awful in these media things or pro-am's, people seriously think I cheat to win tournaments!"

Paired with now-golf announcer Jerry Foltz in the pro-am at River North in Macon, Ga., the week after his 1995 Nike Tour win in South Carolina, we made our way through a few bars afterward and stayed out way too late. (Who knew there was nightlife in Macon?) Decently hungover, Jerry missed the cut the next day.

Other great pro-am partners were Kelli Kuehne at the Chick-fil-A and Brandt Jobe at a Hooters Tour event in Atlanta.

A wonderful bonus was that former PGA Tour and Senior Tour player Greg Powers became a friend and sometimes instructor in the early 2000s. Greg was the victim of a horrific 1992 car crash that easily could have ended his walking days, but he came back miraculously to even play briefly on the Champions Tour. I can't tell you the number of times Greg spent a couple of hours with me and rescued my game.

At another media event, I was paired up with South Korean Aree Song, when she was only 15 and playing in Atlanta's LPGA event, for a three-hole, alternate shot exhibition. I asked the tournament director, Torrey Gane, if I could play with Liselotte Neumann because, well, who wouldn't want to play with Liselotte Neumann?

As a compromise, because the tournament people wanted the *AJC* golf writer to play with the teen sensation for maximum exposure, Torrey put us in the same foursome with the charismatic Swede who, as everyone knows, had the best legs in golf.

"Actually, I wanted to play with you," I told Liselotte on the first tee.

"I would play with you anytime," Liselotte said.

Gulp.

Gathering myself, I drove decently off the first tee.

Pretty good job I happened to have, I decided, walking with Liselotte Neumann down the first fairway.

CHAPTER 34

FURMAN BISHER

U NLESS YOU HAVE LIVED IN THE SOUTH, YOU PROBABLY DON'T realize how huge Furman Bisher was in the business of sports journalism. I didn't realize it myself until I moved to the *Atlanta Journal-Constitution* in 1979 as the *Constitution's* NFL and Falcons writer. Until then, I had only read Furman's stories in the *Sporting News* or occasionally when distributed on the wire services.

It was fine writing to be sure—bold, often bombastic, and always descriptive—but I didn't know anything about the South or Atlanta then. As a result, Bisher's writing never truly hit me until I lived down there with him and around the stories he described every day in his beloved afternoon *Journal*.

Now, here I was, not yet 28 years old and having been in town only a few months, sitting in the press box next to a man who was once named by *Time* magazine as one of the nation's top five columnists.

That distinction was so noted in 1961, and the man ended up writing for more than 50 years longer.

"Judas Priest," as Furman loved to say, for a while he used Shoeless

Joe Jackson as his Facebook profile picture, having once scored an interview with the blackballed man himself.

He's the only man without a green jacket that I had ever seen just barge into the Champions Locker Room at Augusta National, pushing through the old saloon-type doors that once protected it, bellowing, "Hello, Gene! (as in Sarazen)" and never looking back. Had he done so, he would have seen my mouth hanging open in disbelief.

He's the only man who would refuse a request by his Executive Editor to write about Bear Bryant on the day he died, not veering from their long-time feud.

He's the only man who could get away with some of the Old South language he would use in print, or the worse stuff he would say in a press box, shocking many around him. I mention this not to be critical of Furman, but more to demonstrate the depth of his autonomy.

Pity the copy editor who decided to change Bisher's copy without permission from a higher authority. One guy who decided that a colon should be a semi-colon in a Bisher column, legend says, nearly wound up working for the *Siberian Times*.

You expected Furman to be brash, egotistical, and oblivious to whom he might have offended. What you didn't expect was for him to be such a warm, caring person in almost every experience away from his keyboard, when he didn't have to be, well, Furman Bisher.

Few people knew that after retiring from the *AJC* at 91, he wrote for a few very small Georgia papers and didn't even know how much money he was making. Just send it to my church, he told them, and that was it.

But it was Furman Bisher who gave an event in the South instant credibility just by walking into the press box.

When the *Journal* and *Constitution* were "separate" before 1982, the two papers had a strange relationship (also a combined weekend circulation of nearly one million). During the week, we competed against each other to a point but then combined staffs on the weekend. Meaning, you could sit on the other side of the press room from the *Journal* guy all week and try to beat him, then join forces with him on Friday or Saturday, when the papers put out a combined edition.

However, we took the "competition" quite seriously and even one of my sports editors at the *Constitution* used to say, "If you've got something good, either write it Friday night or save it for Sunday night."

I'm only providing a little background here to demonstrate how deeply Furman considered the divide. The *Journal*, he felt, had nothing in common with the *Constitution* beyond the printing press they shared. The *Journal* was conservative, and the *Constitution* was liberal. The lines were clear and without blur.

Furman took it so seriously that each year when we checked into the Media Center at Ponte Vedra Beach, Fla., to cover The Players Championship, the first thing he did was scowl at the nameplate at his seat which said, "Furman Bisher, *Atlanta Journal-Constitution*," and madly scribble a line in black Flair pen through *Constitution*. And the hyphen.

Furman wrote a daily column for some 67 years (subtracting four years in the Navy) from age 20 to 91, first in Lumberton, N.C., then High Point, N.C., and Charlotte, beginning in Atlanta in 1950. The author of more than a dozen books, Furman was still writing when he died at age 93. The following April, at his desk in the Masters Media Center, they placed one of Furman's classic bucket hats, and it stayed there all week, untouched by anyone.

I could almost write a book just on Furman but suffice to say while his image was all curmudgeon, he was truly a softie. Yes, he could bluster as well as anyone, even at the end, but he was a romantic, an emotional father and grandfather and one of the most sincerely loyal and kind friends anyone—even a *Constitution* guy—could ever have.

Only Furman Bisher could write, "You can replace your wife, but you can't replace your putter."

(My wife, Nora, never liked that one, though I always laughed at it, and even told Furman she felt it was inappropriate).

Only Furman would get a knee operation in his 80s so he could keep walking the golf course to cover tournaments. Most guys would just stop walking the course and stay in the press room or retire.

Only Furman could tell Jack Nicklaus that he was leaving the great man's press conference out of respect for his aging kidneys.

Only Furman Bisher, a day after being criticized in his column by the Dodgers' Tommy Lasorda, instead of going down to the locker room at the game's end to confront the manager, could say, "Judas Priest! I don't have time to go downstairs! I've got a column to write!"

Meaning, I don't need Tommy Lasorda for column material. Rather, he needs me.

Only Furman Bisher would have the balls to swivel around in his press box chair after a playoff game to glare at Cowboys GM Tex Schramm and friends loudly celebrating behind him in the Texas Stadium lounge, yelling, "Judas Priest! I've never worked in a fucking nightclub before!"

Only Furman Bisher, then in his mid-70s at the 1994 U.S. Open at Oakmont, could scream at the editor of his paper for its lack of intelligence regarding space commitments, while a group of 20-something writers rooted him on, fist-pumping his every word.

Now don't get me wrong, Furman drove me crazy every once in a while. When we were planning our day's coverage, say, at the Open Championship, and I perchance asked Furman what he might be writing about so we could avoid overlapping, he would usually say, "Oh, just general observations of the day's events."

But sometimes he might say something like, "I'm doing Colin Montgomerie" on a day when the talented Scot had done something very newsworthy and desperately needed to be accounted for in our stories.

Great, I would say, figuring we would be covered, only to find out later that Furman spent perhaps a paragraph or two on him, but then drifted into comments about pretty much anything else that he wished to discuss. Meaning, there were still plenty of holes to fill in the Colin Montgomerie story, so it forced me to discuss him in detail, setting up a troublesome task for our editors. And if somebody was going to get cut because of repetition, believe me, it wasn't going to be the guy who interviewed Shoeless Joe Jackson.

That said, I always felt a need to protect Furman on the road, especially at the major golf tournaments and particularly in Europe, where the electronic challenges with laptops, landlines, or wireless were especially daunting for a guy who started in the business when Western Union was high-tech.

When I would save Furman from computer hell and figure out a way to send his story safely across the Atlantic, he would thank me as though I had just earned a spot in his will.

"Judas Priest, Sheeley, I don't know what the hell I'd do without you!" he would say once again.

Sometimes, though, I was saving the entire media center from disaster, too. At the 1997 Ryder Cup Matches in Spain, the story transmission challenges were formidable. Not only were those bizarre "snake bite" Continental Europe plugs confusing to those accustomed to the standard UK plugs they usually encountered at the Open Championship, but a voltage difference also had been problematic.

(My wife had burned up her curlers in our room to start the week.) Beyond that, it had rained for three days and everything around the place seemed as damp as a leaky cellar.

Anyway, I looked over at Furman's laptop at one point and noticed a small, bluish flame beginning to arc between this strange assortment of plugs he had stacked upon each other and were leading frighteningly into his laptop. Immediately, in mid-sentence, I told him to unplug the mess so we could start over and, well, save the entire building from a short-circuit communications disaster. Eventually, I got him re-connected safely and the world of journalism carried on, completely unaware of the impending doom.

"Judas Priest, Sheeley!" Furman bellowed in relief. "I don't know what the hell I'd do without you. You saved my ass again."

All of our asses, actually, but you're welcome.

And it was my honor, sir, to be there to assist.

CHAPTER 35

ARNOLD PALMER

THE LAST TIME I SPOKE TO ARNOLD PALMER IN PERSON WAS IN the spring of 2005 in his upstairs office at Bay Hill in Orlando, six months before I left the *Atlanta Journal-Constitution*.

I never spoke to Arnold without feeling my late father over my shoulder, pleased to be in the same room with his biggest hero, and this time was no exception.

I was doing a story for the *AJC's* annual Masters section on the 18th hole at Augusta National and needed Arnold's input on it. As you might expect, getting time with Arnold during Bay Hill week is never easy, but his long-time PR man and former newspaper guy, Doc Giffin, made it happen.

Arnold wore a pink cardigan over a white golf shirt, with reading glasses on his nose, and was going through mail at his desk as he greeted me. With him were his wife, Kit, and, of course, Doc.

Because Arnold was always such an unassuming superstar, it prompted me to immediately relate a story I was told by Larry

Dorman, whom Arnold also knew as a Callaway Golf PR man after leaving newspapers.

It involved another sports legend, Arnold's friend, Don Shula. Turns out, one summer Shula and his family were up in Maine for a vacation before Dolphins training camp and a rainy day at the beach had forced the family to the local movie theater.

As Don, his then-wife Dorothy, and the kids filed in down the aisle, a smattering of applause came from the side of the theater. Don glanced over and smiled, gave a little wave, and took a seat on the aisle. A couple of minutes later, when a guy came over to say hello, Shula blurted out, "Gee, I didn't think anybody would recognize me all the way up here."

The guy replied, "Pal, I don't know you from Adam. They said if 20 people didn't show up, they weren't going to show the movie."

The next time I ran into Shula, I told Arnold, I asked him to corroborate the story.

"Yep, that's exactly what the guy said," Shula said, pausing. "You know, you're never as big as you think you are."

Palmer smiled, chuckled, and said, "Did'ya hear that, Kit? You're never as big as you think you are."

Other superstars might have had to regularly remind themselves of that fact, but Arnold Palmer never did. He always was the blue-collar guy on the Pennzoil tractor. Even when playing golf with Presidents. Even yukking it up with Bob Hope on national TV. Arnold always was the guy in the Bay Hill men's grill who would wander over to chat, and it was always a kick when he did.

For both me and my dad.

My favorite Arnold Palmer story is probably the one involving my old Pittsburgh pal, Myron Cope, the nasal-voiced broadcaster who invented the Terrible Towel, waved by those crazy Steeler fans since the mid-'70s.

Before Myron got behind a mike, capitalizing on what he said was "a trend toward obnoxious voices," he was widely acclaimed as a wonderful writer for several notable sports magazines. Well, except for the time, Palmer decided, when he wrote a story for one of them, expressing the opinion that golfers were not athletes.

As it turns out, Palmer, an amazing natural athlete with massive forearms and huge vice-like hands, in 1960 had won the prestigious Hickok Award as the nation's top professional sports athlete. He also happened to be in the bar at Laurel Valley Country Club one day in 1961, when he looked out the window toward the first tee and noticed Cope preparing to hit his drive in a charity tournament.

Palmer ran down the hill to the first tee, and with Cope standing over his ball, said, "Now we'll see how an athlete hits the ball!"

Although Cope often claimed that he easily gathered himself and "hit it right down the middle," he admitted to me, "I was damn lucky to get it airborne."

I could also tell you about the time George Sweda, the former *Cleveland Plain-Dealer* golf writer, took Arnold to his high school reunion, which is true, but I don't have any first-hand details.

I can, on the other hand, relate quite a bit about January 2001, when USGA President Trey Holland came to Atlanta for a supposedly routine luncheon as the Georgia State Golf Association's featured speaker. Instead, he trapped himself into a condemnation of the organization's honorary membership chairman and living legend, Arnold Palmer.

Midway through what was until then a boring speech, somebody decided to ask Holland about Palmer's USGA position and his endorsement of the average golfer's use of the illegal Callaway ERC driver.

Holland's wiser approach might have been to dodge the question, but without hesitation, he said, "We can't have a guy as a visible spokesperson who is championing not playing by the rules of golf."

Undaunted, Holland then said that when people open up their next USGA membership mailer, Palmer's picture will no longer be in there.

So much for boring luncheons. I even asked Holland the question once again after his remarks, giving him a chance to walk it back, but he repeated the quote almost verbatim.

So, I wrote the story, which was big enough to make the sports front of the Sunday paper during Super Bowl week in Atlanta. But before filing it, I tracked down Holland that night after dinner with Georgia State Golf Association executive director Mike Waldron and read the story back to him.

I hardly ever did that, but "This is Arnold Palmer we're talking about here," I told Holland, "and I'd like to get a little sleep tonight if you don't mind."

He asked me to change one meaningless word but was totally fine with his quotes and the story.

Then he went on the Golf Channel the next day, said the story was inaccurate and that his comments were "taken out of context."

While Holland tried to wriggle his way out of what happened, the truth is that he slammed Palmer publicly, acted as though he didn't, and then attempted to blame it on the media (me) for exaggerating it. When he realized his mistake and reinstated Palmer (sort of) a couple of days later, the damage was done.

When I stopped Arnold at Bay Hill two months later, leaving the media center from his annual Tuesday pre-tournament press conference, I related how things went down that night, with Holland confirming the story's accuracy, then turning around the next day and denying it.

Arnold looked at me intently as I went over the details, then folded his arms and said, "That's the first I've heard it that way. This is not over, I guarantee you."

Translation, Arnold was a great guy and a humble man, but he realized how much respect he commanded in the game of golf—and he also knew, quite proudly, that he had earned it.

One year at Bay Hill because of storms threatening to interrupt the final round, tour officials convinced Arnold to send the players off early on Sunday, thereby forcing the telecast into a ratings-dampening, taped-delay format. By mid-afternoon, the skies were still sunny, and I was standing next to a tournament official when a familiar voice came over the radio.

"This is Arnold Palmer," he said. "Where the hell's that weather you were talking about!"

Oops.

Another year at Bay Hill I was there early on a Monday, searching for a Tuesday story, and wandered out to the range, where my friend Billy Andrade was warming up. Arnold was going to play later with Billy, his fellow Wake Forest alum, and walked up as I was standing there, asking about the day's foursome.

"Who do we have?" Arnold said.

Andrade said, "I've got Stewart Cink and Omar Uresti."

"Omar Uresti?" Arnold said, laughing. "I thought he was dead!"

I swear to God, I think Arnold thought he meant Gen. Omar Bradley.

In May of 1967, when I was 15, Arnold made an appearance at Hershey Country Club, where my dad was a member and I often caddied, then later worked in the Pro Shop or on the course. Palmer was playing an exhibition with Australian Bruce Devlin, matching up with Hershey head pro Jay Weitzel and Colonial Country Club pro Phil Bankert.

Arnold was truly still the King then at 37 years of age and, to quote the late Stuart Scott, "as cool as the other side of the pillow."

It was a meaningless match, yes, but positively huge to have him at our home club.

I still remember exactly what he wore. Navy blue pants and black shoes, royal blue cardigan sweater, white shirt, and white visor—and that deep Florida tan. Arnold was truly bigger than life that day for a kid whose state (Pennsylvania) held a special adoration for him. Not to mention, the kid's father.

My dad, Mark, even played those Palmer irons with the thin top line when he couldn't hit them as well as his old Pedersen's—and my dad was a good player. But he liked looking at that Palmer name on them and nobody was going to pry them from his hands. If my dad's bursitis would have allowed a Palmer whirlybird finish, I'm sure he would have treated us to one now and then.

At Bay Hill one year, I asked Arnold if he remembered the Hershey exhibition and he most certainly did—including the fact that Devlin had pumped two balls OB on the par-3 third hole of the HCC West Course, causing gasps from the gallery.

I don't remember a whole lot about the match, but I clearly recall the first hole, a rather short dogleg par-4 that played just east of the chocolate factory, in clear view of the famous mulberry bushes that spelled out HERSHEY COCOA.

Most members would hit either a long iron or fairway wood off the tee there to set up a short iron over Spring Creek to the green. Not Arnold, though.

He pulled out his driver, and lashed a big hook around the dogleg, firing for the green. At the last second, the ball ticked an overhanging tree and dropped into the water, but the effect was still quite dramatic.

Ok, it wasn't Cherry Hills, but Arnold Palmer had gone for the green off the tee at No. 1 of the Hershey CC West Course and almost pulled it off.

That's the Arnold Palmer I'm choosing to remember.

CHAPTER 36

DAN JENKINS

DAN JENKINS WAS ALMOST EVERY SPORTSWRITER'S FAVORITE sportswriter. I was honored to be his friend and it pained all of us to observe his deteriorating physical appearance in the years leading up to his passing in 2019.

When I left the newspaper business in 2005 to take a communications job with The Golf Club of Georgia, Dan sent an email wishing me good luck, and added, "We hate to lose one of the good ones."

That meant a lot to me having read Dan for decades, especially when I first decided to be a sportswriter. He was fall-on-the-floor funny and there aren't many of those guys around.

It was always a kick to stop by his table upstairs in the Masters media center, where Dan, coffee cup and cigarette in hand, would be holding court, usually with Tom Callahan or Dave Kindred or his Texas buddies.

If he nodded and greeted me by name as I walked by, that was extremely cool, too, especially when I first started covering the Masters in 1984. If he came over to my desk to ask a question or to gather background info on a story subject, I felt like the Pope had stopped by for a scripture recommendation.

I must admit, there were a couple of times when I would join the table upstairs and, during the conversation, try out a line I was thinking of using in that day's story. If Dan smiled, it was going to be in the story. If he laughed, I was probably going to lead with it.

We all loved Dan, even those of us who didn't particularly like his hero, fellow Fort Worth native Ben Hogan. His other guys were Palmer and Nicklaus, and that brought us all into the fold.

It's hard to believe how funny Dan was ALL THE TIME. There weren't any slumps. He didn't waste an at-bat. Even Johnny Carson, who had Dan on the *Tonight Show* several times, offered up a lousy monologue now and then, but I can't think of one occasion when Jenkins whiffed.

Even when he wasn't at his keyboard. I will never forget the 2001 PGA Championship at the Atlanta Athletic Club, which was held in Duluth, Ga., in the northeast suburbs. The selected media hotel was the Four Points Sheraton in Dunwoody, about 20 minutes from the course. It was a puzzling choice with so many nice Marriott hotels in the Atlanta area and the PGA of America, especially media relations man Julius Mason, aware that most golf writers considered Marriott Reward points more valuable than a precious metal.

I can only assume the PGA got a media rate it could not refuse, because the hotel was about to be sold and in horrendous shape. Bathroom fixtures were worn out and falling off. The paint was peeling. Remote controls were dead. Hardly the standard anyone was accustomed to from the PGA, which caters to the media like no other golf organization.

Well, Jenkins was receiving an award from somebody on the Tuesday before the tournament, with a press conference being held in one of the hotel meeting rooms to announce it. When Jenkins got to the podium, he could not resist some commentary regarding the accommodations. The nearby hotel workers started smiling as soon as Dan first approached the subject.

"The Four Points Sheraton?" Jenkins asked. "What is that, four points out of a hundred?"

Dan Jenkins changed sportswriting in America, making it irreverent and rowdy and a whole lot of fun.

Did I try to write like him? Absolutely. Everybody did, but nobody succeeded.

There will never be another Dan Jenkins.

I look forward to raising a glass with him on the other side.

CHAPTER 37

SEVE BALLESTEROS

I KNEW SEVE BALLESTEROS ONLY TO HAVE ASKED HIM QUESTIONS in group interviews many times over the years, mostly at the Masters or the 1997 Ryder Cup in Spain, when he captained the European team. He was always classy and cordial, though, and often playfully funny. His quotes in the Masters Media Center are nothing less than legendary.

Perhaps the most famous Seve-ism:

"Seve, how in the world did you 4-putt that green?"

"Well… I mees, I mees, I mees, I make."

"Seve, what do you think about tomorrow after shooting a 70 in the first round?"

"Well, uh, uh, well, uh… eet's Friday."

My favorite Seve story, however, was once related to me by my good friend, Scott Michaux, the former *Augusta Chronicle* columnist. Before a practice round early in the week one year, Seve was stationed on the old Augusta National putting green behind the No. 1 tee box, working intently.

Meanwhile, at the corner of the gallery ropes, near the gate where the players entered and exited, was an excited guy with a deep, country Southern accent who was attempting to get the Spaniard's attention.

"Steve!" he said. "Hey, Steve!"

Irritated, Seve looked up from his putting, glared at the guy, and went back to stroking a few balls.

The guy was relentless. "Hey, Steve!" he said. "Hey, Steve!... Steve!"

At this point, Seve was now either done putting or too distracted to continue, so he walked toward the fellow at the ropes, stopped, and pointed a finger in his face.

"My name is not Steve," he said. "It is Severiano...and your name is asshole!"

CHAPTER 38

GENE SARAZEN

GENE SARAZEN UNEXPECTEDLY ENTERED MY GOLF LIFE AS THE namesake of the old Sarazen World Open, which was played at the Chateau Elan resort in Braselton, Ga., outside of Atlanta, from 1994 to 1998.

"The Squire" was 92 when the resort's owner, Don Panoz, established the event to honor national open champions from all over the world. Sarazen, Sam Snead, and Kathy Whitworth were Panoz's choices to design Chateau Elan's Legends Course, using as "replicas" six of each one's favorite holes around the world.

I had only seen Sarazen at Augusta as an honorary starter a while back during the Masters or hosting those old *Shell's Wonderful World of Golf* matches on TV. But here he was, strolling around in plus-fours, jacket and tie at this very rich tournament, for the time, paying $250,000 to the winner, more than the PGA Tour was handing out then for first place.

It was a very cool tournament, even cold, with 42 degrees one year and 82 the next, which you can get in November in North Georgia.

Ernie Els was the inaugural champion and Frank Nobilo even won it twice. At one time, it appeared as though the tournament was going to be incorporated into the PGA Tour's World Golf Championships, but instead, it merely vanished after the 1999 tournament, held in Spain.

Before that, tournament organizers were trying to see if a different spot on the calendar might work, but it never happened.

I still crack up, though, at a press conference the Tour held with Sarazen to discuss that very issue at Chateau Elan's final Sarazen World Open.

Going through some possible alternate dates in his mind, Sarazen, honest to God, lamented that, for starters, well, "Jones has April."

Jones has April? Seriously?

Jones has April?

Yes, that Jones.

He meant Bobby Jones.

Yes, here was Gene Sarazen, Mr. Double Eagle from 1935, complaining 64 years later about the late Bobby Jones still holding that juicy date on the schedule for the Masters and, well, preventing him from moving his tournament out of November to the spring.

What a classic.

So was an experience my old Atlanta friend, Jim Riddle, had with Sarazen when he was a kid. Playing golf at Pinehurst with his father, they happened to meet Sarazen, in attendance there for a corporate event. Later, when Sarazen traveled to Japan for an exhibition, Jim and his dad received a postcard from him, which they proudly displayed to friends.

Many decades later, Jim Riddle sought out Sarazen at the Chateau Elan tournament bearing his name and re-introduced himself. Sarazen said, of course, he remembered meeting Jim and his dad and even recalled mailing the postcard from Japan. He then said to make sure Jim said hello to his father.

Pausing, Jim smiled and said that his father passed away several years before.

Smiling back, Sarazen said softly, "Well, then I'll tell him hello for you."

CHAPTER 39

PHIL MICKELSON

REALLY TRIED TO LIKE PHIL MICKELSON OVER THE YEARS I covered him. I really did.

I rooted for him to win his first major, at least partially because I was tired of writing about him always coming up short. However, it also made zero sense that Shaun Micheel or Ben Curtis had one of these four cherished trophies and one of golf's all-time best players did not.

I occasionally walked out on the course with Phil's wife, Amy, who is delightful, as we all know.

One day, in between Phil's shots, Amy and I were discussing the importance of being careful when talking about someone on Tour out on the course. Indeed, you never knew when one of Hal Sutton's ex-wives would be within eavesdrop range in the gallery or when a fan might be saying something about, well, your husband.

Amy said she was watching Phil at Harbour Town one year when she heard a woman behind her in the gallery say:

"There's Phil Mickelson. He broke both of his legs skiing and now he plays on two wooden legs."

Amy Mickelson swiveled around at her and screamed, "WHHHAATTT???"

Of course, you must respect Phil's game. That's obvious. The owner of six majors now, he might be in golf's all-time Top 10.

It's the other stuff that I'm talking about.

It's Mickelson ripping Captain Tom Watson while on the Ryder Cup dais after a USA loss, with Tom Watson sitting right there, just a few seats away.

It's Mickelson complaining about having to pay too much in taxes.

It's Mickelson bragging about his game, his gambling, and his abilities in a sport where humility is most cherished.

And, in 2022, it was Mickelson taking huge, controversial Saudi money to join LIV Golf, changing his public image and seriously endangering his place in PGA Tour history.

In other words, it's too much ego and not nearly enough class.

When I was covering golf, Phil's long-time caddie, Jim "Bones" Mackay, was one of my good friends out there. He was always loyal to Phil and never said anything derogatory, but he was a great guy to seek out for inside stuff or his opinion. Typically, we would BS on the range until Phil arrived at the bag, and then I would split. (Never once did Phil jump in and say, "Hey, Glenn, no need for you to leave. Stick around.")

But hey, that's OK. This was his office. Phil was the boss and I still respected him.

That is, until a conversation we had several years after the famous 1999 Pinehurst U.S. Open, won by Payne Stewart.

As you probably remember, in June of 1999, Amy was expecting her first child any day, and because of the delicate timetable, Phil wore a beeper to be alerted if the birth happened before the tournament's end. If so, Phil promised he would leave immediately, no matter where the tournament stood and who was leading. The only speculation among the media involved whether Amy, even if in serious labor, would alert Phil at all, especially if he were in contention.

As everyone knows, the beeper never went off and Payne won on the 18th green with a dramatic par putt, then held Mickelson's face during his celebration and told him, "You're going to love being a father!"

A nice, emotional scene, to be sure.

Phil and I were talking about it on the putting green at Troon, Scotland, during the 2004 Open Championship, just a few months after his first Masters win, for a big feature on him in the *AJC*.

During the conversation, I related to him how, as a young Steelers beat writer for the *Pittsburgh Press*, I had decided to opt out of covering Super Bowl XIII between Dallas and Pittsburgh because our first child was due that week in January of 1979. As it turned out, my wife delivered our daughter Jessica that precise Sunday night, just a few hours after the Steelers' win.

Though such a huge story in Pittsburgh sports history, I never regretted the decision because the birth of your first child is a once-in-a-lifetime experience. As Phil stroked practice putts, I was telling him all the details of my situation, which for my profession, was very similar to his.

It was then that Phil disappointed and shocked me all at once with his response.

"It's not the same at all," he said. "You're talking about covering something for a newspaper. I'm talking about winning the U.S. Open. It's not anything like what you're telling me."

I think I mentioned to him that, well, it was the most important thing in my world at the time, same as in yours.

"No, it's not the same at all," he said. "It's not even close to the same thing."

I've never looked at Phil Mickelson the same way since. I was in disbelief that even if he felt that way, he would be so rude and uncaring as to say it so coldly.

It was one thing that we writers often jokingly called Phil "Eddie Haskell" because his insincerity reminded everyone of the old "Leave it to Beaver" character, but this was different. This was Phil being full of himself and lacking any ability to empathize with what I went through. Which blindsided me completely, or else I wouldn't even have mentioned it to him in the first place.

I've told this story to a lot of my friends and colleagues over the years, and each time I get a "You've got to be kidding! What a jerk!" response from them, or worse.

Maybe I've let it bother me more than has been warranted over the years.

But, then again, maybe not.

Come to think of it, I bet it would bother Amy Mickelson, too.

CHAPTER 40

MOM & GARY PLAYER

M Y MOM, JANE, WAS ALWAYS A BIG GARY PLAYER FAN AND SHE even kept one of his instructional books on her nightstand.

One year when I was covering the Nationwide Championship Senior Tour event at the Country Club of the South in Alpharetta, Ga., I was on the range at mid-week searching for a story when I heard a fan approach Player with a request.

"My dad is a big fan of yours and he's dying of cancer," the guy told him. "Could you say hello to him for me?"

Player obliged without hesitation. He grabbed the fellow's cell phone and chatted with the man for probably five minutes or so. It was impressive.

If I ever get a chance like that, I told myself, I'm going to find a way for Gary Player to talk to my mom. She would go absolutely nuts, I was certain.

Fast-forward to maybe a year later, when during a rain delay at the same tournament, Player had wandered into the media center to make a phone call. He happened to grab a phone immediately to my right and started talking.

I'm doing it, I told myself.

I asked Gary if he wouldn't mind saying hello to my mom, who is a big fan, and he said, "Certainly, laddie, I'd be happy to."

So, I called her on my phone and said there was someone here at the tournament who wanted to say hello. I didn't tell her it was Gary Player because I wanted her to be blown away by it, so I handed him the phone and Gary started babbling away in his delightful South African accent.

"Mrs. Sheeley, it's so wonderful to speak with you," he said. "Your wonderful son tells me you are a big fan and I just wanted to …"

Then he stopped talking because my mother was asking him a question.

And that's when Gary Player said to my mother, "Noooooh, it's not Greg Norman" and identified himself.

Oh, my God, Mom. You've got to be kidding. Embarrassed? That didn't come close to describing it. I told Gary I was sorry and then told him again, but he just smiled and told me not to worry about it for one second.

I've got to admit, never once did I even ponder that Gary Player's voice would be anything other than unmistakable, even to my mother in her limited Pennsylvania small-town world, where apparently any foreign voice sounds pretty much the same, whether it's from Australia, South Africa or Edinburgh.

Suffice to say, I never attempted something similar again. Unfortunately, FaceTime, which probably would have been sufficient for my mother to make a positive ID, had not yet been invented.

CHAPTER 41

QUEEN ISABELLA

THIS CLUSTER OF SHORT TAKES IS ENTITLED "QUEEN ISABELLA" as a tribute to one of my old composing room friends, Bill Cooper, at my college newspaper at Penn State, the *Daily Collegian*.

When newspapers finally progressed to the "cold type" format, which involved shooting a page photographically and creating a negative, as opposed to rolling the ink over a bank of lead pieces, now you could read it normally, rather than right to left and upside down.

So, when a story came up short with this new format, you could see immediately that a paragraph or two, or maybe just a few lines, might be needed to fill the column hole. These were called shorts or fillers, and it was easy to stick them on the page.

Maybe it was a paragraph that, say, listed Willie Mays' lifetime averages. Or maybe it was a game result that had been cut from a longer story. Sometimes there were several shorts stuck on a composing room board next to the page in progress, often supplied by the *Associated Press*, ready to be used if needed.

Or, if you were Bill Cooper, it was often a slightly gnarled, somewhat yellowed piece of photo paper that he kept in his wallet for just such occasions, ready to put it once again through the waxer and stick it to the page.

Bill's short read simply:

"Queen Isabella enjoyed hunting wild boars."

Obviously, our readers could have continued their lives without knowing this tidbit of information, being quite a reach as a sports item, but this never bothered Bill, and he used it regularly. Then, when the page was shot and sent to the printers, Bill peeled off "Queen Isabella" and stuck it back in his wallet.

My "Queen Isabella's" are much longer and surely would not fit in Bill's wallet, but I hope you enjoy them.

I was assigned to cover a celebrity charity tennis match in the 1980s at the University of Georgia in Athens, Ga., featuring singer Kenny Rogers, who had a massive farm near the college, former Secretary of State Dean Rusk (a UGA grad), and actors Pat Harrington, Jr., and Christopher Atkins.

At the time Kenny Rogers was known for his hit song, "The Gambler," and was also a part owner in a United States Football League team, the Houston Gamblers.

Steve Eubanks, the author, and I were among a few reporters speaking to Rogers after the match. Among other things, we discussed the USFL's marginal financial situation.

Never one to pass up a smart-ass line, I asked Rogers about the Gamblers and inquired:

"Are you going to know when to fold 'em?"

The other writers cracked up at the reference to his hit song.

Rogers did not, just staring ahead and never answering. The interview broke up shortly afterward.

Hmm, you picked a fine time to leave me, Kenny.

Most people know Tony Dungy as a Hall of Fame NFL head coach and TV analyst on NBC. I will always remember him as a rookie Steeler defensive back in 1977 when I covered the team for the *Pittsburgh Press*.

Tony had such a feel for the game that you assumed he was destined to be coaching at some point. He was so studious that while most of his Steeler teammates were napping or watching soap operas on TV in between two-a-day workouts at training camp, Tony was often stationed in his floor's common room, watching film.

The coaches loved it. His fellow players loathed it, irritated that Tony's projector was ruining their TV reception.

Before Tony's time with the Steelers was over, he would accomplish something no player since the AFL-NFL merger has ever managed. Entering a game against the Houston Oilers on Oct. 19, 1977, as Pittsburgh's "emergency" quarterback after injuries to Terry Bradshaw and backup Mike Kruczek, Dungy became the only player ever to throw an interception and catch one in the same game.

I was cleaning golf clubs at my summer job in the pro shop at Hershey Country Club before my sophomore year in college when one of my high school buddies, Glenn Laudermilch, came by, gushing to tell me something.

"You're 308, " he said.

I didn't have to ask. I knew he was referring to the draft lottery, and I had received a number that, thank God, ended any fears of being forced into the military. Anything over 150 was reasonable assurance that you wouldn't be marching at Fort Dix in a few weeks.

You can have your 59s. To this day, 308 remains the best number I ever heard at a golf course.

In the late '60s, I qualified for the Pennsylvania state high school golf tournament at the Hershey Park Golf Course, which required leaving class early to make my tee time. Because I needed a caddie and really couldn't afford one, I asked one of my high school friends, Wayne Paul, to carry my clubs in the one-day, 18-hole tournament.

And that's all he was, a bag carrier. Wayne had never caddied and surely just did it to get out of class, but it helped my fatigue factor on a very hilly, tricky course.

I was playing OK and had a chance to break 80 with a birdie at the last hole, a dogleg left par-4 which demanded that the caddies walk far ahead to spot balls flying overhead.

Sadly, though, when I got to my drive, I saw that my ball was positioned in the back of a divot.

"I can't believe it!" I groaned. "Of all the luck."

Whereupon, Wayne said, "Oh, you should have seen it before. You wouldn't even have been able to hit it."

I swiveled back to him and said, stunned, "WHATTT!"

As it turns out, Wayne had been moving the ball and improving my lie all day, totally unaware that in tournament play, unlike how it might be with your buddies in winter or early spring in Pennsylvania, you play the ball where it lies.

Shaken by this news, I intentionally hit my second shot into the creek, made double bogey and thankfully missed the cut.

When I started working for The Golf Club of Georgia after leaving the *Atlanta Journal-Constitution* in 2005, there was always talk of the glory days at the upscale, 36-hole private club in the early 1990s, when it was Japanese-owned, and the membership fee money was flowing. Several of the owner's high-roller friends from Japan wanted to join and thought nothing of writing a check for $52,000.

After a few weeks, an employee in the accounting department was stunned to open an envelope from a new member that contained another check for $52,000 and immediately called the gentlemen for an explanation.

As it turns out, the man was so accustomed to clubs in Japan requiring hundreds of thousands of dollars for private golf privileges, that he thought $52,000 was The Golf Club of Georgia's fee for monthly dues,

Yes, that's somebody with far too much money, I would have to agree.

For a brief time in 1992, because the "Sportscene" column I was writing several times a week for the *Journal-Constitution* had become popular with our readers, managing editor John Walter asked me to take over the Features Department's "Peach Buzz" around-town column, hoping to add some life to it. I wasn't thrilled because it meant at least temporarily leaving the Sports Department, but there were a lot of perks. I was single at the time and there was no shortage of invitations to plays, restaurant openings, and assorted parties.

This included regularly covering a nightclub called Petrus in midtown Atlanta that frequently gave out its "Petrus Nightlife Award" to various unique celebrities. Julie Newmar, who played "Catwoman" in the "Batman" TV series, was one of the honorees, prompting Petrus to serve us a private dinner in cat dishes. Tula, a transsexual woman formerly named Barry Cossey, was invited to attend one night. And so was Zelda Rubenstein, who played the exorcist in the movie, "Poltergeist."

Well, let's just say that Zelda and I didn't exactly hit it off. I had written a story advancing her appearance and listed her as 78 years old, according to the Petrus press release. Turns out, there had been a typo in the info that had been faxed to me, and she was actually only 58. When I was introduced to Ms. Rubenstein late in the evening, she claimed I had damaged her career.

"What career?" I asked.

The exchange earned me *Atlanta* magazine's "Best Retort" of 1992, but at what price? I had angered the only exorcist I ever knew personally.

My role as golf writer at the *AJC* and later doing publicity with The Golf Club of Georgia allowed me to play golf with some interesting celebrities.

The most unlikely one was Father Wilton Gregory when he was Archbishop of Atlanta. If you think that's strange, then also picture him out of his silk robes and wearing Oakley sunglasses and a Cleveland Golf visor.

Michelle Hiskey of the *AJC*, Father Gregory, and I were playing the Creekside Course at The Golf Club of Georgia when at the 15th hole two notable things happened.

First, Father Gregory bladed a wedge that hit a rock in the creek and almost cleared the water, prompting me to call this, "The Immaculate Deflection."

(I admit, I had prepared this line beforehand, hoping I would get a chance to use it.)

Then Father Gregory spotted a fat water moccasin in the creek while hitting his next shot. Deciding it to be "the sign of the serpent," he figured that to be enough strokes for one hole and picked up his ball.

I was playing in a charity scramble with Bonecrusher Smith, the heavyweight boxer who had fought Mike Tyson, when our foursome was having trouble making birdies. After two of our partners missed, I declared, "Let's see what the Bone Man can do."

Instead of putting, he glared back at me.

"You don't like that name?" I asked carefully.

"NO!" he said, tersely.

"In that case," I said, "Good luck, Mr. Smith."

My wife and I got to know Jane Seymour, the actress, through Nora's store in Roswell, Ga., Elegant Attic, where she carried the Jane Seymour Collection of sheets, scarves, pillows, and artwork.

In the process, we also got to know her then-husband, James Keach, who produced *Walk the Line,* the Johnny Cash movie.

You might not know that James was also an actor and had a famous role in the comedy classic, "Vacation."

If you remember the scene when Chevy Chase forgets that he tied the biting dog to his bumper and is stopped by the motorcycle cop holding the leash and demanding that he get out of the car, well, that cop was James Keach.

The cop famously asks, "Do you know what the penalty for animal cruelty is in this state?"

"No, sir, I don't," Chase says.

"Well, it's probably pretty stiff," the cop replies.

Fast-forward to me taking Keach to play golf at The Golf Club of Georgia during the week of Jane's appearance at the store. On the fifth hole, James had to take a drop for an unplayable lie, managed it kind of sloppily, and I couldn't resist.

"Do you know what the penalty for an illegal drop is in this state?" I asked him.

Laughing, he said, "No, sir, I don't."

"Well," I said, "it's probably pretty stiff."

CHAPTER 42

FAVORITES

MY FAVORITE STORIES TO HAVE COVERED:

- The 1986 Masters—The 6th green jacket for Jack Nicklaus.

- My car trip from Los Angeles to Danville, Calif., with John Madden in 1986.

- Jack Nicklaus' final British Open at St. Andrews in 2005.

- The Ernie Holmes cocaine possession trial in Amarillo, Tex., in 1977.

HONORABLE MENTIONS

- The 1997 Masters—Tiger Woods' first and the most socially meaningful.

- The Atlanta Braves' 1992 NLCS win over the Pirates—The Francisco Cabrera hit, the Sid Bream slide, and five continuous minutes of bedlam.

- Jean van de Velde's collapse at the British Open at Carnoustie in 1999. (I always regretted calling him "The Claret Jughead" in my game story. It was a good line, but a little cruel. I genuinely liked the man.)

- The 1994 U.S. Open at Oakmont—Arnie said goodbye and O.J. was arrested on the same bizarre Friday afternoon. (A break-even day, as it were, for Hertz Rent-A-Car, which employed both of them in its commercials).

- Braves owner Ted Turner's only game as a manager after firing Dave Bristol in 1977, losing at Pittsburgh, 2-1.

CHAPTER 43

TWEETS

AFTER I RETIRED FROM THE DAILY BUSINESS OF SNARKY commenting, I usually resisted the urge to go on Twitter with something to say about sports events—or even occasionally something political—but sometimes I couldn't help myself.

(5/21/14) "Christine Brennan calling Michael Sam (who came out as gay) the most important football player in the nation is the least important thing written this year."

(3/26/14) "Sad day for golf with the passing of our pal, Ron Balicki. Nicest man ever in the golf writing business and honored to have been his friend."

(2/22/12) "If writing headlines with off-color puns was a firing offense 20 years ago, a lot of us would have been in the insurance business."

(2/13/12) "Phil has outperformed Tiger on Sunday before, but

I can't ever remember him dressing cooler than Tiger. White shoes with black pants is a bogey."

(5/2/11) "Apparently no truth to the rumor that as the attack happened, bin Laden was in his compound watching a re-run of 'Undercover Boss.' "

(10/2/20) "Pence says Trump is 'well at this time.' That's odd. He wasn't well before he tested positive."

(9/2/20) "Was with Beano (Cook) for a Penn State game at Annapolis one day and he was reading off names on the stadium façade across from us. 'Marshall Islands...Iwo Jima...Wow, what a schedule! And they're all on the road!'"

*(10/7/19) "Remember when people tuned in to **Monday Night Football** to hear what the announcers had to say and often what they said was big news? How the hell can such a famous TV booth give us nothing better than Tess & Booger?"*

(9/30/19) "As Ukrainegate evolves, yet more evidence appears on a daily basis that someone who hosted a 'reality show' in fact knows absolutely nothing about reality."

(5/27/19) "A fast-food junkie with no interest in working out, Trump (pictured with a Sumo wrestler) decides on the easiest solution to improve his physical image—do photo ops next to fatter people."

(1/28/19) "HELLO!! When is the NFL going to realize that a Super Bowl city should avoid any city where cold or snowy conditions are possible, if not probable? Clearly, SB visitors want to spend the week in mild temperatures! Sadly, the NFL only picks sites to award owners for new stadiums."

(6/2/18) "For a guy who could be called for an offensive foul nearly

every time he drives, LeBron is doing an awful lot of bitching over a block that, by the way, was the proper call!"

(5/13/18) "When Trump met the prisoners released from North Korea, it reminded me of the freed Iranian hostages being given a lifetime pass to Major League Baseball and the legendary Beano Cook asking, 'Haven't they suffered enough?'"

(2/21/18) "I know I'm not going to vote for these guys from the juiced curling era. No way."

(1/21/17) " 'Pep in his step… hits it a country mile….eats them alive'………Did Kelly Tilghman (on the Golf Channel) just set a 5-minute PGA Championship cliché record?"

(7/30/16) "Donald Trump says, 'The gloves are off.' If I were Hillary, I would be sure to point out that 'as we all know, they are very small gloves.'"

(7/22/16) "Write-in vote is the only sane solution this November. I'm going with the Jeff Foxworthy-Kathleen Madigan ticket."

CHAPTER 44

TV FUN

G IVEN A DECENT VOICE AND NEVER ONE TO REFUSE A CHANCE to gab, I had done some radio stuff over the years, hosting a sports talk show on the old WGST Newsradio in Atlanta or joining FM morning hosts Gary McKee, Christopher Rude, and the late Rhubarb Jones mostly for laughs, but until the Golf Channel emerged in 1995, I didn't have a strong urge to try anything serious on TV.

Not only was the Golf Channel connected with Arnold Palmer, which automatically made it cool, it looked fun and exciting, so I decided to pursue getting involved with it.

Having been covering the PGA Tour for a year or so, I had gotten to know some of the Golf Channel personalities and was very intrigued when Peter Kessler started his *Viewer's Forum* show featuring media people he felt could offer an insider's view.

Through my friend Jennifer Mills, one of the Golf Channel's original on-air people, producer Lee Siegel responded, and I was booked for a show with Peter in the summer of 1996. The network paid airfare, meals, and lodging at Bay Hill (no cash compensation), but later the *AJC* would provide a small promotional fee to reporters for that type of appearance.

I didn't really care. Staying at Bay Hill, there was always a chance of running into Arnold at breakfast or later in the grill, and just being around a golf-only network in its infant period was a blast. Plus, Peter and I hit it off splendidly from the start. His golf knowledge was staggering, and he was incredibly gifted at making his guests the stars of the show. Peter appreciated that we were taking the time and effort to be there, and he wanted his viewers to get to know us.

During our pre-show meeting, if I happened to be telling Peter a story he particularly liked, he often stopped me short of the ending or the punch line, preferring to hear it live on the air for the first time so his reaction would be more genuine. I was stunned that he trusted me enough to deliver it live, but the story usually came off better that way, as Peter suspected it would.

Surprisingly, I was relaxed, given how little experience I had doing live TV, but there were a few moments when fear temporarily struck. You know how it is, say, at a party, when you might be telling a story or a joke, lose your train of thought, and have absolutely no idea what the next sentence might be emerging from your mouth? Well, take that feeling and multiply by 100 when it's live TV.

While it can be quite a rush knowing that you're about to say something to a few hundred thousand viewers and you can't be edited (like in a newspaper, for example), it can also work the other way, too. You can't let your mind wander, even for a second, because at that exact time, the host might say, "Glenn, what are your thoughts on that?" and you might start flop-sweating like Albert Brooks in *Broadcast News*.

Fortunately, that never happened, and the free TV gig soon turned into a paying one when Jim Huber, my late friend at CNN &

Turner Broadcasting, asked me to join his CNN/SI show, *Golf Plus*, as its PGA Tour insider. I was flattered that Jim would ask me and thrilled that an opportunity presented itself across the street from the *AJC* building, as opposed to flying to the Golf Channel studios in Orlando.

I did one *Golf Plus* show in the CNN studios with Jim, who was moving over the Turner's TNT network, with veteran Bob Fiscella then taking over as the main host. Bob and I became good friends over the years, first at CNN/SI, then later at The Golf Club of Georgia after I left the *AJC*, when he agreed to host our TV highlight shows for both the Georgia Cup and the United States Collegiate Championship. It's hard to find people in the TV business with a great voice and a minimal ego, but that was Bob all the way, and he helped me become more comfortable with every show.

I was never very clear on the exact viewing audience for *Golf Plus*, but it was bizarre to be occasionally given an example of the show's global reach. An Australian media buddy, Bernie McGuire, told me he watched the show while sitting in his hotel room in Frankfurt, Germany. I also had a few South African friends who were regular viewers.

Occasionally, the show was broadcast on CNN International when there wasn't adequate satellite time available on CNN. While it didn't make much difference in the show's content or format, I remember one day we were in the middle of taping when the studio lights suddenly went out and we were shut down. Turns out there had been a bombing somewhere in the Middle East and the CNN people covering important news needed the satellite for a live broadcast.

It was somewhat of a revolving door with the show. I worked with nine different hosts, including Kyra Phillips (currently with ABC News), Laura Okmin (FOX), a soccer dude from Argentina named Pedro Pinto who barely knew a 4-iron from a waffle iron, and

London-based Patrick Snell, who had this weird habit of pulling on my jacket or sleeve to force me into a tighter camera shot.

The gig lasted for a couple of years, providing me with some recognition and beer money. It also allowed me to regularly explain PGA Tour insights with some accuracy and behind-the-scenes expertise, rather than trusting the soccer guy from Argentina.

With Bob Fiscella going to FOX Sports Southeast when CNN/SI folded up as a separate network, he asked his bosses to use me on some remote stuff from tournaments in the U.S.

At least partially, I must admit, I jeopardized my newspaper duties with the FOX Sports Southeast work, specifically in 2005 at the U.S. Open in Pinehurst. In my defense, though, I was close to moving on at that point and getting increasingly miffed by the political moves taking place within the *AJC* sports department. Otherwise, I'm sure I wouldn't have left the press center in the middle of my game story to sprint over to the 18th green for my TV spot with Bob and FOX Sports. As it turned out, there was no harm done despite being away from my computer for a half hour, but I wasn't comfortable, and I never allowed myself to be pulled between the two tasks in that manner again.

Live TV, of course, always has the potential for unusual developments, and even with my brief involvement in it, I witnessed a few.

I remember one instance while working with Tom Rinaldi, who became quite a star with ESPN and FOX. He was at CNN/SI back then and was asked to do a live shot with me at the 2001 U.S. Open at Southern Hills Country Club in Tulsa. We were positioned off a fairway near the clubhouse, with no shade and temperatures over 100 degrees. Had we spent 10 more minutes out there, I think we'd have developed heatstroke. There was so much sweat pouring from us, that you'd have sworn that one of the course sprinklers had sprayed us.

One CNN/SI live shot at The Players Championship with a

storm approaching nearly became a total disaster when a huge gust of wind grabbed an umbrella attached to the set and hurled it toward us in the middle of our report. But with his right hand remaining steady on the camera, unfazed veteran CNN cameraman John McAfee spotted the flying umbrella from the corner of his eye, grabbed it with his free left hand, and miraculously kept it out of the shot, much to our producer's relief and amazement.

When I reflect on those early days of the Golf Channel, I can't help but think about my pal Tim Rosaforte, who died tragically at only 66 of Alzheimer's in 2022. Tim and I appeared on some of those *Viewer's Forum* shows together and played a lot of golf on the road, often with Bob Harig, then of the *St. Pete Times,* and the late Steve Hershey of *USA Today.*

Tim was the working model for transitioning from print to TV and became its first real golf insider. He was a great guy and worked harder than anyone in the business. He could take a call from a source while standing over to putt. He carried two cellphones before anyone else ever thought of it and occasionally you could find him in the press room with one to each ear.

I could always make Tim laugh with a quick joke. I wish to God I still could. Every time I see my old Golf Channel friends Rich Lerner or Steve Sands at the occasional tournament I attend these days, it makes me think of Tim.

Lerner's Golf Channel piece after Tim's death was one of the most touching things I've ever seen on television, and Rich is one of my favorite people in the golf TV business, and not just because he's always a good audience for my Hubie Brown and Al Davis impersonations. Rich is a writer first, and the words he delivers on air are more descriptive and passionate than those from almost everyone else.

Lord knows he's been good for my career, too, frequently pulling out lines I used in stories and repeatedly quoting them on the air more than a decade later.

Several times on Golf Channel telecasts Rich has repeated my line at the 2005 Masters, when I called the gritty Chris DiMarco, who lost in a playoff to Tiger Woods, "tougher than a Waffle House porkchop."

That was a newspaper line, mind you, not from a Golf Channel appearance. The excitement of TV notwithstanding, I always knew where I belonged.

CHAPTER 45

LIFE AFTER NEWSPAPERS

WHEN I LEFT THE *ATLANTA JOURNAL-CONSTITUTION* IN 2005, the newspaper business was certainly changing for the worse. The internet became the new priority and print was struggling for attention, and I didn't want to be around when it bottomed out. I always said you either leave newspapers or they leave you, and it was a lot easier doing it on your terms.

I also always imagined that if a PR job with a great golf club ever materialized, I would jump at it, and I was relating as much to my old pal, Jeff Paton, one day on the phone. Jeff was then Director of Golf at The Golf Club of Georgia in Alpharetta, Ga., and I had developed a good relationship with everyone there over the years covering events such as the Georgia Cup and the PGA Tour's senior event, the Nationwide Championship.

What could be better, leaving the daily grind of the newspaper business and getting full golf privileges at a club I could never afford to join? Not to mention, being part of a genuine team at a major golf club with a national reputation, planning and publicizing events with my extensive media contacts.

So, Paton created a job for me, and I left, ending a 26-year stay at the *AJC* and 32 years in the newspaper business by taking a job at The Golf Club of Georgia as Director of Business Development.

Truthfully, the job title was a little exaggerated, which Paton had a reputation for doing. It was more of a communications and public relations position, which was fine and very relaxing for the most part after more than 30 years of deadline pressure. The business aspect of it mostly consisted of gathering sponsors for our two events, The Georgia Cup (our annual pre-Masters match between the reigning U.S. and British Amateur Champions), and the new United States Collegiate Championship, which from year one would become one of the most popular events in college golf, attracting all of the best teams, including many from the West Coast who made the USCC an annual stop.

(A footnote here is that Paton and Georgia Tech golf coach Bruce Heppler originally wanted to call it the Collegiate Masters, but I quickly informed them that the guys in green jackets down I-20 would have a problem with that. Hence, the United States Collegiate Championship was created at a table of the Men's Grill by Paton, me, and Heppler.)

For the first three years, the job was perfect. I played a lot of golf, sometimes entertaining clients or potential sponsors, but often treating my old newspaper buddies to a great lunch and equally splendid golf on either our Lakeside or Creekside course. I'll never forget that first time I went out by myself to Lakeside shortly after taking the job. I striped a drive on the par-5 first hole, nailed a 4-iron, pitched onto the green, and barely missed an 8-foot birdie putt. I took a deep breath and realized, "Man, I'm getting paid to do this!"

I worked hard for those two months before each of our two events, handling PR and creating our official programs, but the rest of the time it was pretty easy. I had a great office overlooking Lakeside and could pretty much name my hours. I ate lunch off the Club menu every day and enjoyed our social events, including Nora in them when I could.

It got even better a year into it when we moved from Woodstock 35 minutes away to the Windward subdivision of Alpharetta, which included the golf club, and slashed my commute to five minutes. The property taxes and HOA dues were much higher, but it was worth it to be at work (or on the course) in no time, with a view of Lake Windward.

I loved working with the Georgia Cup competitors. From the moment the British and U.S. Amateur titles were acquired and the players officially qualified for our match, they were my responsibility. First, I had to make sure they were committed to attending our event the week before the Masters, and then I had to physically get them to Alpharetta, Ga.

It wasn't always as easy as you might think. I remember when Brian McElhinney of Ireland won the British Amateur in 2006 at Royal Birkdale and I had to locate him, FedEx him some official Georgia Cup apparel, and firm up his travel details. This was the address I had for him:

Brian McElhinney
Burnfoot
Donegal
Ireland

No house number. No postal code. That was it.

When Brian walked in the front door of the club that next spring, wearing his Georgia Cup shirt and carrying the FedEx box, I considered it nothing less than a miracle. He ended up beating U.S. Amateur champion Edoardo Molinari of Italy, who became a good friend with whom I texted or emailed over the years.

In 2007 Colt Knost, who won the U.S. Amateur at the Olympic Club near San Francisco, was to play British Amateur Champion Drew Weaver of Virginia Tech in the 2008 Georgia Cup match. The two players couldn't have differed more greatly.

Colt was classically Texan, brash and cocky. Drew was friendly, polite, and humble and looked like a USGA poster boy. But I liked both of them immensely. After all, it wasn't Colt's fault that his agent was disrespecting our charity event and misrepresenting his client. In other words, being an asshole.

It was a challenging week, to say the least. For a while it looked like the match wouldn't happen since Knost had controversially turned pro after the Walker Cup matches that summer, even forfeiting his spot in the Masters. Not only did his agent insist that Colt wear his normal Titleist garb instead of using our Georgia Cup apparel and bag, but because Colt was committed to playing a Nationwide Tour event in California that week, the agent demanded that we guarantee his arrival there by Monday night to compete in a Tuesday pro-am.

To accommodate this situation, we agreed to move the match from Tuesday to Monday and make sure Colt got to the airport Monday night. Because we couldn't guarantee to avoid Atlanta's infamous traffic jams during rush hour, we decided to lease a helicopter to pick him up on the range and take him to Hartsfield-Jackson Airport. Fortunately, Colt had just won the match, which meant at least we weren't giving the loser this luxury treatment. To even things up a little, we gave Drew a limousine ride to Augusta on Tuesday.

Our United States Collegiate Championship was just as big of a kick for me. While the USCC tournament committee usually made the team selections, sometimes I got to do it myself, even making the call to a very excited golf coach.

Surely, I could have retired in this position, were it not for one major thing.

The Golf Club of Georgia's shaky financial picture finally caught up to it a few years later. The club was on the verge of bankruptcy, partially because of a ridiculous mortgage from its original member purchase and a lot of reckless spending.

It got so bad that a few of us were furloughed for several months and then only brought back when the club was in foreclosure and entertaining new buyers. It was a mess and it worsened when Ben Kenny became the new owner, eventually getting rid of most of us. I understood, having been around new head coaches who cleaned house to bring in their people, but the way Kenny did it was totally classless.

Telling me that "family was everything," he approved a trip to Dallas in June of 2014 to see my new grandson, Luke. As it turned out, the uneasiness I felt while leaving town was warranted.

I returned to discover that Kenny's people had cleaned out my desk and closet and boxed everything on top of the desk. I was given a small severance check that came nowhere close to approaching my lost membership income, but at least I was through with this guy and felt a bit of relief.

After a few months with my own consulting and communications business, I was able to land the Membership Director position at Hawks Ridge Golf Club in February 2015. Although Hawks

Ridge wasn't nearly as busy as The Golf Club of Georgia and demanded a commute of 35 minutes, it was a chance to work for the club that existed previously as my most serious competition.

I will never forget John Smoltz, the Braves Hall of Famer, spotting me as he came off the 18th green and jumping out of his cart to welcome me to Hawks Ridge with a firm handshake. A former member at GCOG, he was now playing most of his local golf at Hawks Ridge and was excited about what I could bring to the membership effort. Along the way, he brought me a couple of new members himself, including Chipper Jones, his former teammate.

Hawks Ridge was more of a boutique club than GCOG, with far fewer rounds and members. But if you didn't mind nearly $800 in monthly dues, you were able to play a great course, with outstanding food and hospitality, and privacy you could not enjoy anywhere else in the Atlanta area.

Eventually, I also got some other big-time athletes to join, such as Paul Millsap and Kent Bazemore of the Hawks. We displayed their jerseys, along with Smoltzie's, in the locker room, and it was an impressive statement when walking prospective candidates through the clubhouse.

I stayed there just over two years, right after we hosted the U.S. Open Sectional Qualifying in 2017, thankful for the opportunity, but tired (at age 66) of taking orders from anyone or being required to show up for work at a particular time.

So, after nearly 40 years in the Atlanta area, Nora and I moved to Ormond Beach, Fla., in December of 2018, less than an hour's drive from Orlando, my daughter Jessica and husband Jeff, and our two grandsons, Tyler and Bryan.

I watch the boys play in their U.S. Kids golf tournaments far more than I play myself, I swim in my pool almost every day, and

I enjoy the weather and Florida lifestyle with Nora. I watch golf on TV and read the Daytona Beach paper and the *AJC* on my phone.

I don't miss the newspaper business, but I miss the people.

I'm glad I got to be a newspaperman when newspapers still mattered.

And it was better than lifting things. Really.